This book does not happen without my partner in life and in practice, the one true love I always believed in: my wife Heather.

This method has blessed our connection with real intimacy. I wanted the design to reflect the beauty of that blessing—because my goal is for you to experience it too. Well, Heather has an "oh pretty!" radar I completely trust. So, page by page, she made sure the book sparked that reaction.

Heather also has this uncanny ability to track with instructions. Early in our relationship, when I'd give her instructions I believed were well thought out, she'd notice flaws that I didn't. So Heather also brought that superpower to this book: making sure you're guided through the Truth Empowered Relationships method logically, smoothly and consistently. Our intention is for you and your relationship to get the most benefit possible from the concepts you're about to read.

Most of all, this method doesn't exist without Heather. Because even though I spent two decades learning and practicing the world's most transformational personal growth technologies, I never found someone who wanted to live a mutually conscious life. From our very first conversation—during which Heather amended answers to my questions to be more truthful—she's been dedicated, as I am, to making sure our relationship is always fully transparent and psychologically responsible.

We've gone through some tough challenges. But even through the toughest, Heather always inspires me. She sees being alive as an opportunity to grow. She embraces the rainbow of emotions that is life in human form. And she radiates love: even in the exceedingly rare moments when I don't enjoy what she's saying or doing, I always bask in the precious glory of her energetic presence.

Heather made this book beautiful, and my method real. And every day, she makes my life worth living.

TO HEATHER

TRUTH EMPOWERED RELATIONSHIPS

REAL INTIMACY THROUGH CONSCIOUS HONESTY

WRITTEN BY
MARSHALL ZWEIG

EDITED AND PRETTIFIED BY
HEATHER MASSON

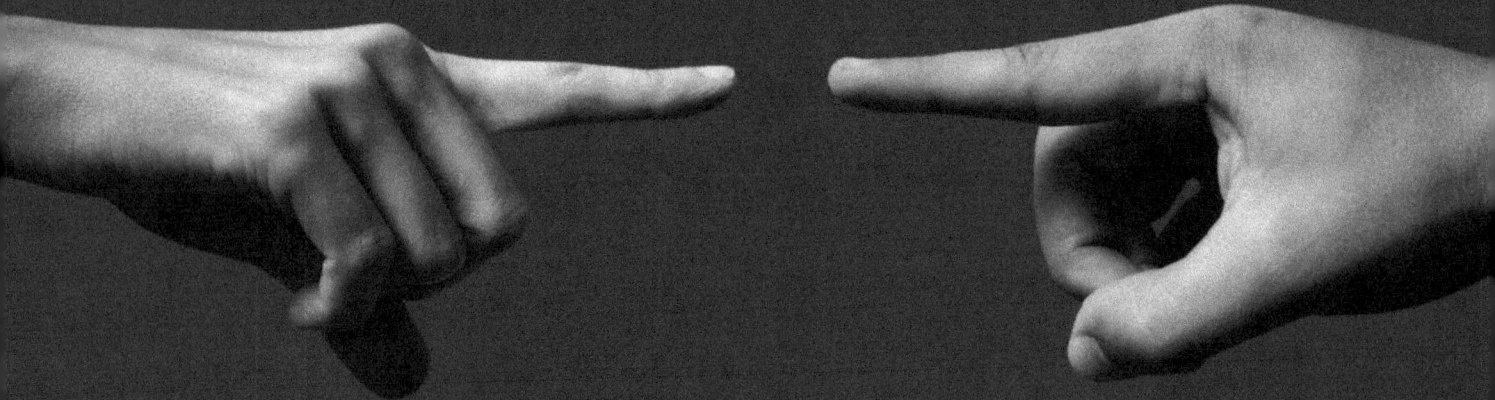

IF THINGS FEEL DIFFICULT RIGHT NOW, EVEN IMPOSSIBLE...

I PROMISE YOU,

I understand.

This is a revolution in intimacy: a method that will radically transform how you experience love.

It's rare people reach for a book like this when all is well. If you're having challenges, even major ones, I promise you: I've felt that pain. I've made that desperate search for a solution. It's why I created this book.

Let me share my relationship challenges, and how I overcame them—with this method.

We all watch a movie through our eyes. We're the star, we're the narrator, but the people around us get all the screen time. As kids, many of us watch movies with arguments—sometimes cruel or even violent ones. The adults in your movie might've talked against each other, divorced, battled in court. Many of you were even put in the middle of those battles.

Moments from our movies often replay in our adult relationships.

In my movie were parents who truly loved each other. Watching their relationship was the most beautiful and also the most psychologically safe element of my childhood. I was fascinated by it, and I noticed everything about it—including ways I would have said and done things differently to create even *more* intimacy.

But I struggled for decades to find my special someone. Childhood sexual trauma had a lot to do with it. So did my indoctrination of codependency —caring about others' feelings but not my own. But, determined to experience real love during my time on earth, I spent two decades learning the world's most transformational personal growth technologies, studying the patterns that create both harmony and disharmony in love. That hard-earned wisdom is why I'm with my soulmate. It's also the source of this method. You see, I now know why love so often suffers, languishes and dies: it lacks a framework that nurtures intimacy.

That's this method—a structure that makes it psychologically safe to love without walls and masks. Because no matter what movie you've been watching, having fulfilling relationships can be the most challenging and elusive part of life. As proof: the U.S. Surgeon General declared loneliness an epidemic.

Be careful who you let coach you. Make sure they live what they coach. Heather and I live a Truth Empowered Relationship. I've also forged non-romantic ones with my son, mother and closest friends: deep, rich, warm connections full of openness, honesty and acceptance. In my life and in my coaching, I'm a stand for the truth.

Truth Empowered Relationships take bravery and commitment. They aren't easy. But they can also be fun and exhilarating—and they're designed to make your love deeply intimate.

That's what I wish for you: the deep, fulfilling intimacy we all need, crave and deserve.

Hello, I'm
Marshall

FIND ME AT **MARSHALLZWEIG.COM**

"*Communication* TO A RELATIONSHIP IS LIKE *oxygen* TO LIFE. WITHOUT IT, IT DIES."

—TONY GASKINS

Table of CONTENTS

Truth Empowered Relationships
In brief

THE CONCEPT

Being in a relationship can bring up our **triggers**: unresolved inner conflicts shaped by past experiences. When the relationship is intimate, those inner conflicts *are bound to get activated.*

Truth Empowered Relationships enables you to navigate these activations with grace. You're protected from mistreating each other, committed to each other's well-being, and able to have convos that can heal. Quite literally, you'll be your own source of transformation.

THE PROCESS

This method is structured so you'll have fun as you learn. The seven levels blend playful games with practical insights, helping you uncover hidden dynamics in your communication, and understand the patterns and possibilities that shape your connection.

By the end of this workbook, you'll have clarity about how your inner world meets and responds to your partner's. Your relationship will be fueled by authenticity, curiosity, and mutual care.

Welcome to
TRUTH EMPOWERED RELATIONSHIPS

This is no ordinary relationship. This is complete and total intimacy.

Truth Empowered Relationships is a unique method of conscious communication that lets you truly love and be loved in return.

A Truth Empowered Relationship isn't always comfortable, or easy.

It's always real.

COME TO TRUTH EMPOWERED RELATIONSHIPS   WELCOME TO TRUTH EMPOWERED RELATIO

This workbook will guide you through mastering Truth Empowered Convos: a structured, shared language of conscious honesty that creates profound and authentic intimacy. Each level explores key aspects of mindful dialogue—backed by neuroscience and psychology—along with interactive tools and innovative games. By the end of this book, you'll be equipped to dramatically deepen the intimacy in your relationship.

You'll gain a richer understanding of your inner world, and how you process life. You'll be able to communicate that inner experience with clarity, sensitivity and respect, and listen to your partner's with supportive, curious neutrality. You'll learn to recognize and gracefully navigate the subtle emotional landscapes and sensitivities that shape your interactions.

In short, you'll be an intimacy expert.

LEVEL

01

TRUTH AND SENSITIVITY: THE FOUNDATIONS OF REAL CONNECTION

19 PAGES + COMMITMENT

LET'S DO IT!

What you will learn

There's unshakable trust when your relationship's grounded in truth and sensitivity. Being honest in a relationship takes being connected to your emotional core—or reconnecting to it. Let's practice tuning into the truth and sensitivity that will fuel your shared language of authentic intimacy.

"EMBRACE YOUR *inner* WORLD. LET IT *fuel* YOUR CONVERSATIONS."

—MARSHALL ZWEIG

WHY WE *limit* CONVERSATION AT FIRST

Let's talk about why I recommend you don't talk much right now.

Most couples seek out relationship coaching because their communication feels broken. When your connection's strained, conversations can quickly turn into misunderstandings or arguments. So with Truth Empowered Relationships, we'll take it slow. Instead of jumping straight into deep or charged conversations, we'll start with small steps, teaching you how to speak and listen consciously.

I know that certain conversations about practical matters are necessary for couples to have. Other than those, though, I ask that you intentionally scale back your exchanges for now, to help avoid potential miscommunication or conflict while you're still learning the process. We'll focus first on building the core skills: noticing, Truth Empowered Speaking and Truth Empowered Listening. Think of it as learning a new language that will help you connect better—not just with your partner, but also with yourself.

Along the way, you'll also find internal prompts, designed to help you become more aware of what's going on inside you. If you're not tuned into your inner world, you're likely to feel lost or frustrated—and more likely to be reactive. That's why we'll spend time strengthening your inner awareness, so when you do talk, it's from a place of clarity.

This method helps you **resensitize**: tune back into your emotions, your intuition and even the world around you. Resensitizing deepens your ability to understand yourself and your partner. This kind of awareness results in real intimacy.

Once you've built up these skills, we'll reintroduce conversations step by step. By then, you'll have the tools to communicate with clarity, sensitivity and mutual respect. Your exchanges will be richer and more meaningful. You'll have a deeper understanding of yourselves and of each other.

For now, I encourage you to each keep a journal, for your private reflections on the prompts ahead.

To CONTEMPLATE

Contemplations are opportunities for you to explore your honest feelings without the need to filter or explain them.

Write down your 'stream'—your inner truth —about the contemplation prompts. Keep your answer private for now; this is your space to reflect freely.

- **What will it be like for you to limit conversation with your partner?**

- **Will it be a challenge? A relief? Both? Something different?**

WHAT'S *truth* GOT TO DO WITH IT?

Let's explore the concept of truth in a Truth Empowered Relationship. What is it? What are its components? Why is it essential?

Study after study says a truthful life enhances mental and physical well-being. One University of Notre Dame experiment divided subjects into two groups. Only one group was told to stop telling any lies for 10 weeks. The no-lie group reported improved health, less tension and sadness—**and improved personal relationships**.

While the experiment highlights the power of honesty with others, Truth Empowered Relationships takes this concept one step deeper—into the realm of self-truth.

As human beings, we have an innate desire to express ourselves: to share our thoughts, feelings, senses, reactions and stories with others. But we learn not to. We're corrected or scolded for what we share, told to be positive, to not complain, to suppress emotions others find uncomfortable.. Some may blame us for their reactions to our honesty. Some may even try to talk us out of what we experience with our own senses.

We learn to withhold and lie—even to ourselves.

I know all too well the damage lying to myself did to my relationships and mental health. Simply put, someone who's lying to themselves has no chance for a truly intimate relationship. An essential component of intimacy is knowing and expressing your inner truth, so you can *be authentic*—share who you really are. But you can't share who you really are if you don't know who you really are. That's where this method begins: getting us back in touch with our truth.

Science tells us honesty is essential for having thriving relationships. A Truth Empowered Relationship requires an unwavering loyalty to the truth, internally and externally. Without truth as your foundation, intimacy becomes a facade, an illusion, instead of the fuel that creates genuine connection. That genuine connection starts with ourselves: we must notice, express and learn to accept the parts of us we don't know and don't like— because knowing and sharing ourselves is what creates the deepest, most authentic connections with others.

To CONTEMPLATE

- What's your relationship to the truth?

- What truths about yourself do you avoid, suppress, resist, or deny? Why do you feel the need to hide from them? What might you discover if you faced them?

- What truths are you withholding? What might you have to feel in order to share them?

- Where do you feel tension between who you are and who you think you 'should' be?

- What would it feel like to live in full alignment with your true self?

WHY IT'S WISE TO *resensitize*

Desensitization is commonplace and insidious. It's also debilitating to intimate relationships.

From a young age, we're conditioned—often by well-meaning people we trust—to suppress or avoid emotions that are considered uncomfortable or painful. From overt phrases like "you're too sensitive" to seemingly harmless ones like "cheer up" or "look on the bright side," we're subtly encouraged to detach from our true feelings. Even common questions like "how are you?" can divert us from gleaning the wisdom in our emotions, and instead, evaluating them as good or bad.

That evaluating disconnects us from our inner world—and from the people we love. Studies show emotional awareness is what lets us respond with empathy. When we're desensitized, we lose the ability to empathize. If one or both of you are desensitized, the breakdown in empathy can cause your relationship to fail.

Suppressing emotions can dull the responsiveness of the **amygdala**, a brain region critical for processing feelings. Over time, this suppression impairs our ability to experience and respond to emotions effectively. That leads to numbness or heightened anxiety.

Resensitizing is the antidote. It's the quiet alchemy of feeling yourself back to life—letting emotions wash over you, not as enemies to conquer but as messengers to embrace. The process sparks **neuroplasticity**, the brain's miraculous ability to reshape itself.

Imagine carving a path through an unexplored forest: you start with an overgrown trail. But with each step and each swing of the machete, the path becomes clearer and easier to follow. That's neuroplasticity. In the same way, opening to emotions forms new neuronal pathways that bring clarity. So resensitizing is more than self-improvement; it's self-reclamation.

Giving yourself permission to feel fully again reattunes you to your own feelings and needs, and to the subtle symphony of others'. Each act of courage—leaning into discomfort, naming what's real—etches new grooves of trust, connection, and empathy in your brain. You open the door to deeper relationships, richer careers, and a life that feels less like survival and more like magic.

So how do we resensitize? By developing our ability to notice our own state of being in any given moment—the first step to feeling fully alive.

_To_ CONTEMPLATE

- What's your relationship with sensitivity?

- Were you desensitized? If yes, in what ways did it shape your emotional world?

- What fears or beliefs come up for you when you imagine allowing yourself to feel openly?

- In what ways might fully reconnecting with your sensitivity transform the way you experience your closest relationships—including the one with yourself?

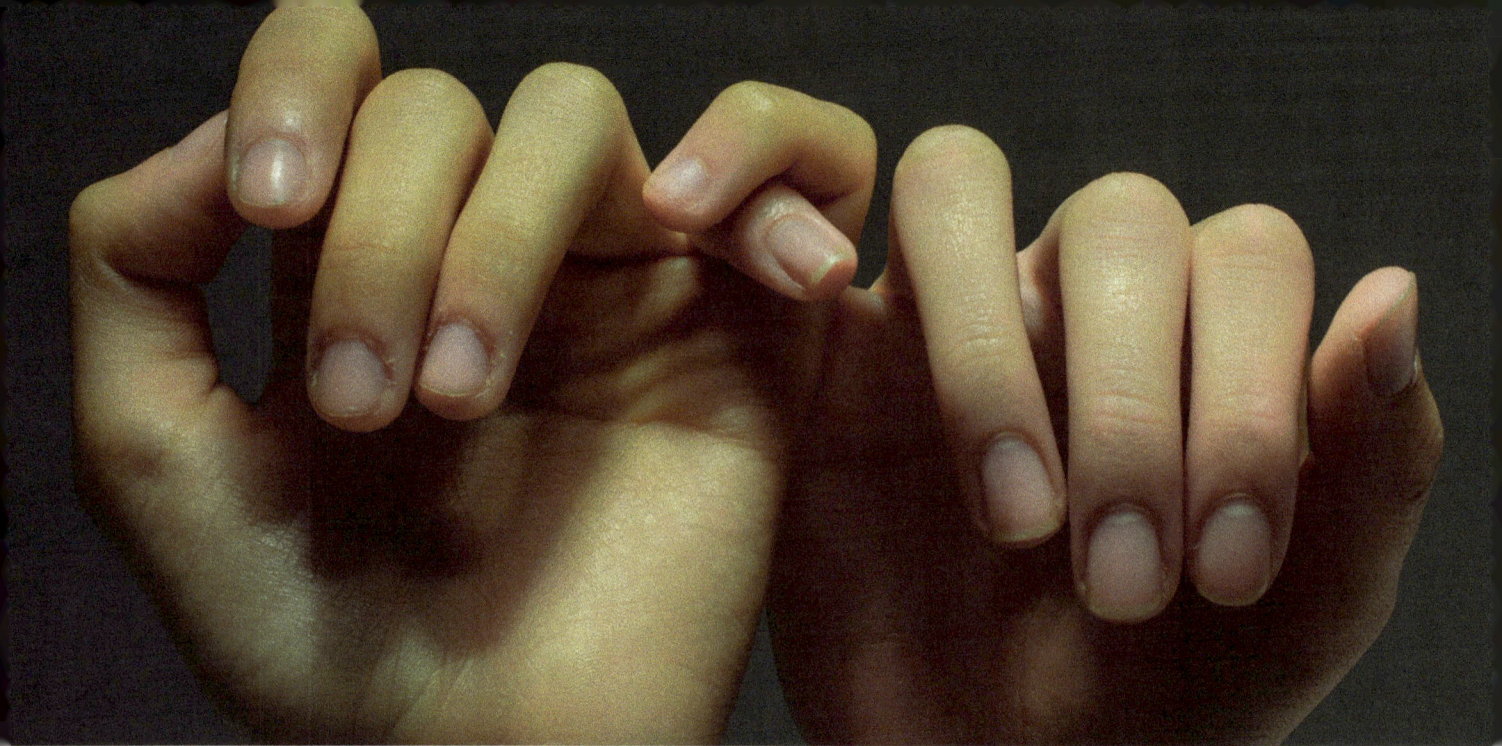

Committing to a life of
TRUTH AND SENSITIVITY

Committing to a life of authenticity means leaving behind the identities we form to gain approval, keep love, or get ahead in life. These identities often feel like our 'winning formula.' But even when they bring us what we want, there's a problem: we can't fully enjoy or appreciate what we've achieved, because we've compromised who we are.

WHEN WE COMPROMISE WHO WE ARE, WE COMPROMISE OUR EXPERIENCE OF LIFE ITSELF.

We often learn in life that *familiarity breeds contempt:* showing our true selves can be risky. In a Truth Empowered Relationship, we say *vulnerability creates intimacy*. That may seem intimidating if being vulnerable has led to pain, criticism or rejection. But in this method, vulnerability isn't just safe; it's cherished. Being fully open, even when it's difficult—*especially* when it's difficult—is honored.

When you're completely honest, regardless of the outcome, you're being true to one person above all: yourself. So *vulnerability creates intimacy* is the guiding principle of a Truth Empowered Relationship—because no matter what, your vulnerability creates intimacy with *you*. When you stay true to you, the love you get is real, because it's given for who you really are. That's real love.

Its foundation is threefold:

- Embrace the full spectrum of emotions, without avoiding the discomfort of pain.
- Learn a **shared language** of conscious honesty, so you can communicate your inner world in a way that creates safety and understanding for you and your partner.
- Heal not just ourselves, but also our partner, through this connection.

In Truth Empowered Relationships, we share with sensitive honesty, and listen without judgment. It's a language that acknowledges both of your humanity, and makes both of you an integral part of each other's development.

OUR
Commitment

As you move through this workbook, you'll have opportunities to reflect and make sure conscious intimacy is what you want for your relationship. For now, are you willing to commit to exploring together? If you are, consider the following words as commitment starting points:

- We commit to living authentically, even when it feels vulnerable.
- We commit to learning to share our truth with integrity and compassion.
- We will practice sensitivity, learning to acknowledge our feelings without judgment.
- We choose a relationship that honors truth and sensitivity, creating a safe space for us to grow and connect.
- We commit to setting aside intentional time (I recommend 30 minutes, 4-5 times per week) to progress through this workbook together.

A COMMITMENT TO TRUTH AND SENSITIVITY IS MORE THAN A ONE-TIME DECISION. IT'S A DAILY PRACTICE.

"A journey of a thousand miles begins with a single step." —Lao Tzu

Reconnecting
TO YOUR TRUTH

ASK YOURSELF QUESTIONS

Consistently exploring your inner world strengthens your intimacy muscle—and your relationship with yourself. To start, ask questions like 'What *might* I be feeling?' and 'What's causing me to feel that way?'

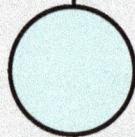

BEGIN TO DEVELOP YOUR ABILITY TO NOTICE

Tune into the details of your inner world. You may notice internal dialogues you haven't noticed before, like thoughts debating your emotions or decisions. This is normal—and it'll be useful as we progress.

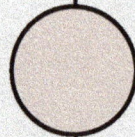

GET OUT OF THE PARADIGM OF GOOD OR BAD

When you view feelings and experiences through a binary lens, you push away 'bad' feelings and cling to 'good' ones. This hinders growth. Instead, embrace the full spectrum of your life, without judgment.

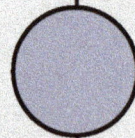

BECOME AWARE OF YOUR TENSION

Note the subtle shifts caused by tension. Does tension increase, decrease, or stay the same around this person? In this environment? Your answers may reveal where you're suppressing or ignoring your inner truth.

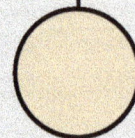

TRUST THAT YOUR TRUTH MATTERS

Many of us hold in, push down, or deny our truths, believing that withholding them keeps us safe. **Your truth matters**. Only you experience life in your unique way. You honor yourself when you share yourself fully.

Reconnecting
TO YOUR SENSITIVITY

SENSORY FOCUSING

Focus on one sense for 60 seconds at a time. Hear even the faintest sounds. See the slightest visual details. Rub thumb and forefinger together until you feel the ridges. Exercise each sense daily and notice what you discover.

NOTICE EMOTIONAL SELF-INVALIDATION

Notice when you minimize your emotions, with phrases like "I shouldn't feel this way," or when others do it, with phrases like "You're overreacting." Pause, step back, and gently reconnect with what you're truly feeling.

HONE YOUR EMOTIONAL SPECIFICITY

Practice naming your feelings and needs with greater precision. Instead of "I feel bad," ask: am I frustrated, lonely, anxious? You'll deepen self-understanding and improve communication. A helpful resource: cnvc.org

REMOVE LABELS

Describe an object without naming it. For example, put a coffee cup into words without calling it a 'cup:' use its texture, weight, color and feel. Removing labels helps you connect with the essence of what you're observing.

CHECK IN WITH YOURSELF

Schedule moments during your day to ask, "What am I feeling right now?" Pausing to check in with your current emotional state strengthens your self-awareness, and helps prevent you from suppressing emotions.

Relationships
as a game

I'm asking you to think about relationships as a game. But I recognize that many people seeking relationship support may be in a tough emotional place. Playing a 'game' when you're in this place may feel counterintuitive; it may not seem to meet your relationship where it's at. But neuroscience shows that games can transform relationships.

Games create structure around interacting, which can turn overwhelming or adversarial dynamics into something manageable—and even joyful. They encourage cooperation, creativity, and emotional regulation.

Games promote **interbrain synchrony**: during shared activities, people's brainwaves sync up because of shared focus and mutual prediction. Interbrain synchrony is like dancing in perfect rhythm, or solving a puzzle together. Synched brain activity creates harmony and mutual understanding, even when you're tackling challenges.

Playing games also activates the brain's reward system, releasing **dopamine**, which gives you a sense of achievement and well-being while it reduces stress. With structured, playful interactions, couples can shift their emotional experiences and create space for positivity, collaboration and growth—even during difficult times. *Psychology Today* says viewing relationships through a game-playing lens can develop trust, and help you find more constructive approaches to overcoming conflicts.

Finally, consider a powerful principle of neurolinguistic programming called **reframing**. It says the meaning you give something isn't fixed—it's flexible. Reframing is like moving from the driver's seat to the passenger seat in a car: you're still on the same road, but now you're seeing it with less pressure and more curiosity. So for example, failing a test might mean you're not good enough—or you can choose to see it as a learning opportunity. The same applies to relationships: when they're reframed as a game, new possibilities emerge that didn't exist before.

Simply put, game-playing can be a transformational tool for relationships.

So let's get ready to play our first game.

Most of the games in Truth Empowered Relationships require a Player 1: someone to 'go first.' I suggest you choose who's Player 1 by playing Rock Paper Scissors. Here's the neuroscience behind my request.

Rock Paper Scissors actually engages critical areas of the brain associated with decision-making, strategy and pattern recognition. By playing this simple game, you exercise both the **prefrontal cortex** (responsible for higher-level thinking) and the **basal ganglia** (which supports habit formation and pattern recognition).

As you try to predict your partner's next move, you're also engaging in what neuroscientists call **theory of mind**: the ability to understand another person's thoughts and intentions. This strengthens the neural networks involved in empathy and social cognition.

In addition, the hand gestures activate the motor cortex, while the need to quickly choose a response enhances executive function. Together, these processes boost problem-solving skills, reinforce strategic thinking, and encourage mental flexibility.

And you thought it was just a kids' game! The thing is: *it is*. The idea is to get back to the childlike wonder of living life with an open heart.

So every time you need to decide who's Player 1, engage your brain and your heart with Rock Paper Scissors. Best two out of three wins.

The neuroscience behind
rock paper scissors

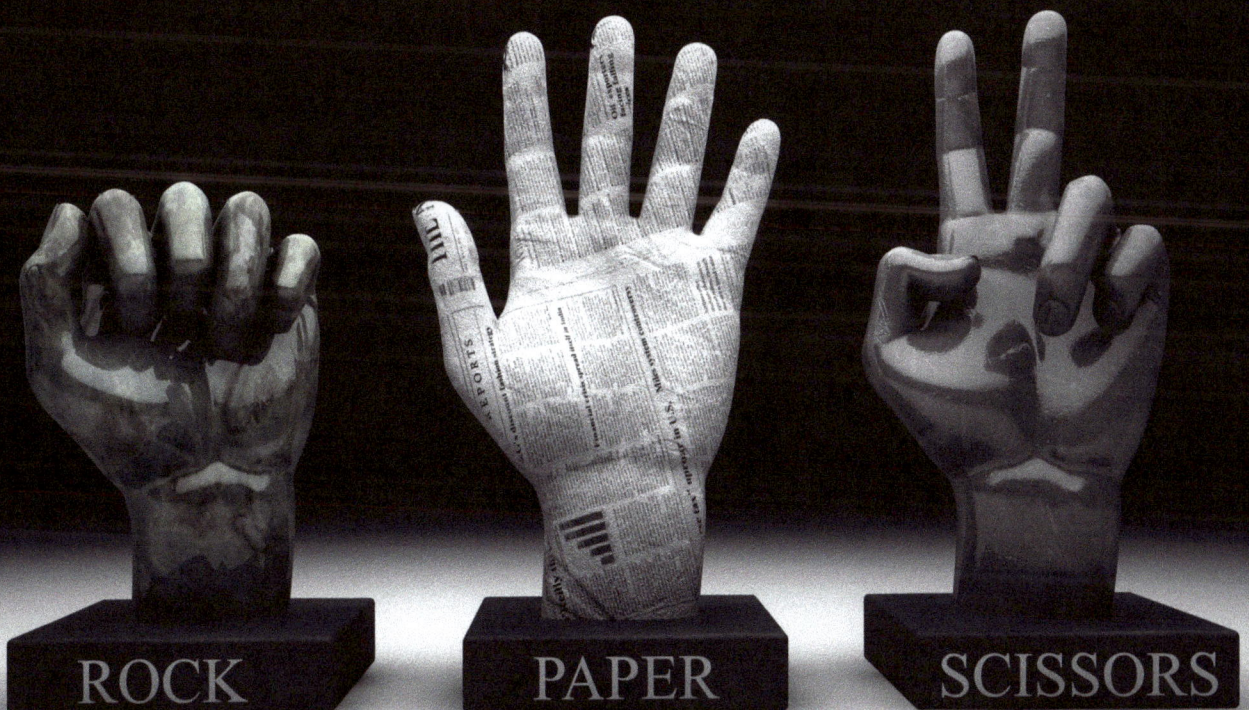

ROCK   PAPER   SCISSORS

it's time to play

INTERNAL WEATHER REPORT

Where you share what it's like to be you in any moment

INTERNAL WEATHER REPORT

FOR 1-2 PLAYERS

SUGGESTED LENGTH 2-3 MINUTES

OBJECT OF THE GAME

Build emotional awareness and strengthen your connection to your inner reality by regularly checking in with your own and your partner's internal states.

Play this game for four days. In addition, read one of the following four pages each day. Then **advance to Level 02.**

HOW TO PLAY

With A Partner:
Play Rock Paper Scissors; the winner is Player 1.

Player 1 shares their "Internal Weather Report," a description of their current internal state. It can be metaphorical: "It feels cloudy in here," or "I feel stormy." It can also be something like, "I'm preoccupied with this, worried about this, I can't believe this person said that to me..."

Player 2 simply witnesses the other's report, without trying to change or fix it. After all, **you can't fix the weather!** Allowed responses: "Got it." or "I heard you." or "That makes sense."

Switch roles, with the second partner now offering their internal weather report and the first partner witnessing.

Solo Play:
Set up to 3 alarms during the day. When the alarm sounds, pause and ask yourself, "What's my internal weather report?" Then tune in. Over time, this practice builds self-awareness.

"LOOK INSIDE YOU FOR THE ANSWERS. YOU'RE THE ONLY ONE WHO KNOWS *what's best for you.* **EVERYONE ELSE IS JUST GUESSING."**

— CHARLES DE LINT

We're just starting to express ourselves. Maybe it's easy for you to share face-to-face—many people get energized by eye contact, and by forming and speaking their stream in the moment. But you may find that other ways to communicate better support your vulnerability.

Maybe you need more time and space to find your words. Then live-messaging or texting from different rooms can be a powerful alternative. Texting lets you interact in real-time, but with the option to reflect and reword your responses. If speaking aloud works but visual contact doesn't, try voice calls or voice texts.

If you prefer physical presence without direct eye contact, try looking away as you speak, focusing on a fixed point, or closing your eyes. Sitting side-by-side or back-to-back also gives you physical closeness without eye contact.

The point is, vulnerability with a partner doesn't have to be one-size-fits-all. Feel into what way feels best for you. Then ask for that style when you need it. Knowing and asking for whatever style works best for you honors *you*.

Honoring *your* communication style

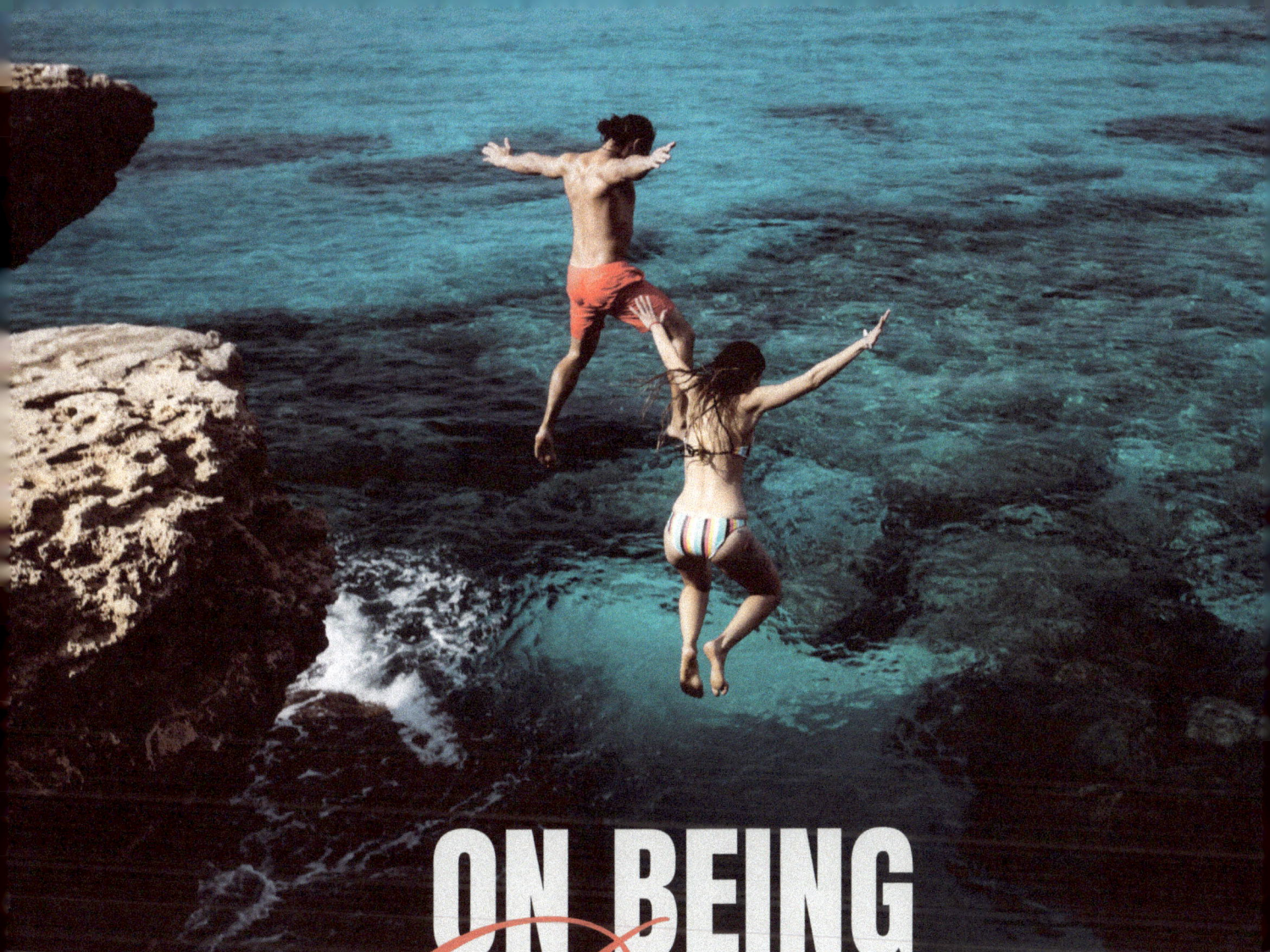

ON BEING
Brave

For many of us, being vulnerable in relationships feels like standing on the edge of a cliff—heart racing, unsure of what lies below. Letting someone into your inner world means exposing your fears, insecurities and dreams.

That takes bravery.

Vulnerability challenges our ancient instincts to shield our soft spots. Saying, "Here's my rain, my thunder, my sunlight, with no filters," means risking rejection, getting unwanted advice, or even triggering your partner—and all of these outcomes carry the possibility of pain.

Yet despite these risks, opening up rewires our brain for trust and intimacy. That's why Brené Brown famously calls vulnerability "the birthplace of connection and joy." Revealing yourself turns walls into bridges.

It takes courage to admit a fear, confess a mistake, or open up to emotions you'd rather avoid. But daring to be seen, flaws and all, allows you to be loved not despite your humanity, but because of it. To open up is to show that love is stronger than fear—and that's the bravest act of all.

A NOTE ON
Unwinding

Unwinding is a relationship's easiest hack

In *Internal Weather Report,* one of you shares what it's like to be you in that moment, while the other holds space—accepting, non-judgmental, attentive space. It's a form of **unwinding**: giving someone the space to simply listen to themselves, find their own clarity, and sometimes uncover answers they didn't know they had.

Unwinding lets us access our inner wisdom. When someone listens to us intently without judgment, it activates the speaker's **default mode network (DMN)**, a group of brain regions responsible for self-reflection, memory consolidation, and pattern recognition. When the DMN is engaged in a safe, supportive environment, thoughts and feelings surface naturally, giving rise to organic insights. Unwinding also creates a sense of safety for the speaker: compassionate listening has been shown to reduce stress responses in the body, which can allow the speaker's true voice to emerge.

Unwinding doesn't require special skills—just presence, patience, and an open heart. In a world of quick fixes, toxic positivity, and "just get over it" advice, someone simply listening can be a refreshing shift. When the topic isn't about the listener—just life, work, or whatever's in the speaker's consciousness—unwinding helps them hear themselves, leading to understanding, clarity, and calm.

And yes, it can be challenging when the share *is* about the listener, and we'll get to that. But for those everyday moments, letting someone unwind is a simple hack that will level up your connection.

*T*ension is more than stress. It's your body whispering, "There's a message here."

Often, that's the whisper of an unprocessed experience. When the nervous system perceives a threat, your limbic system, your brain's emotional HQ, reacts before your conscious mind can catch up. The emotional charge of a feeling you couldn't process fully—a heated argument, a sudden loss, a harsh critique, a time you wanted to say "no" but somehow couldn't—gets stored in your body, often showing up later as chronic tightness or pain: stored tension.

Trauma can create stored tension. Danger or emotional overwhelm can cause your **autonomic nervous system** to activate the **acute stress response**—often called 'fight or flight'—to protect you. But if you can't fight or flee, you may freeze, leaving an unresolved charge in your body.

Tension as an Opportunity

Here's the good news: tension isn't the enemy. It's an opportunity. By finding your curiosity about it, you can help your nervous system finish what it started and release the emotional energy it's been holding. Just like unwinding thoughts can lead to clarity, unwinding tension lets you connect with and rewrite unspoken narratives that may have been silently shaping your reactions—and impacting your relationships.

The process begins with noticing your tension. Instead of brushing it aside or powering through it, tune into it with curiosity. .Then start unwinding it, by asking:

- *What's under the tension?*
- *What feeling is trying to surface?*
- *What would this tension say if it could speak?*
- *What story have I told myself about this tension?*

Your Body Knows

If you're used to ignoring discomfort, unwinding may feel strange. But as you practice, you may notice something incredible: *your body knows how to heal.* That tightness in your neck, that clench in your gut—they're signals, pointing you toward emotions waiting to be felt, processed, and released.

Think of tension as a knot tied by an old story. Unwinding the story gives your body permission to untangle that knot, leading to serendipitous insights and new clarity.

Next time you feel your jaw clench or shoulders tighten, be curious. Give your tension a voice with your *Internal Weather Report.* You might discover tension isn't a block—it's the key to your transformation.

Do you notice tension? If you do, what might it be about?

Tension:
the stories your body holds

LEVEL

02

LET'S GO!

KNOWING YOUR TRUTH: THE POWER OF NOTICING	13 PAGES + WORKSHEET

What you will learn

You'll discover, without judgment and without attachment, all the ways 'you be you' in your inner world. You'll meet each facet of your personality, and develop your connection to your unique voice. You'll exercise that muscle of noticing, which will increase your ability to create intimacy and depth.

"SEEING THE *small*  IS CALLED *clarity.*"

—TAO TE CHING

The benefits of
DEVELOPING YOUR ABILITY TO NOTICE

Paying attention to your inner world—your emotions, thoughts, impulses, the bodily tension we talked about—is like holding the map to your own wisdom. It helps you navigate life with clarity and grace.

When you're unaware of what's inside, your brain can misinterpret harmless moments as threats, triggering stress responses and emotional chaos. Ignoring your inner signals is like walking through a field of hidden landmines.

But noticing changes everything. Tuning in without judgment engages your prefrontal cortex, quieting the amygdala's alarm bells. As your body realizes there's no real danger, the **parasympathetic nervous system**—a network of nerves that helps the body relax—steps in, guiding you back to calm. You can unlock the wisdom tucked within your emotions, because their potential intensity has been defused.

Spiritual traditions and neuroscience agree: awareness leads to transformation. When you allow yourself to fully experience what's inside, without trying to fix or escape it, you not only build emotional resilience, but you also connect with an endless fountain of intimate information, that can strengthen and deepen your relationships while it guides your own way forward.

The more you practice noticing your inner world, the easier it becomes to create richer, more meaningful connections by sharing your authentic self with others.

Noticing
YOUR INNER WORLD

FEELINGS

Feelings come before thoughts and shape our experience. Notice them, and the thoughts they inspire, without judgment.

THOUGHTS

Thoughts arise to help process, understand or respond to our emotional world. Notice them with curiosity, not criticism.

JUDGE | SABOTEURS

Recognizing these inner voices can offer valuable insights. To learn more about them, visit positiveintelligence.com

REACTIONS

Reactions to sensory data can seem to overtake us. Noticing these reactions can lessen or even eliminate their power.

MEANINGS

Nothing has inherent meaning. We assign meaning based on our perception. Question the meanings you assign to things.

RESENTMENTS

Resentments form when needs aren't met. Notice and express resentments consciously, and you can resolve inner tension.

STORY IN OUR HEAD
***vs.* INTUITION**

Intuition is an inner knowing, while stories in our heads are shaped by patterns and beliefs from past experiences. When our intuition is repeatedly invalidated, we may confuse the two.

WANTS AND NEEDS

Maybe we didn't feel safe asking for what we want or need. Maybe we didn't know *how* to ask, or that we *could* ask. Separating from wants and needs can harm relationships. Let's reconnect with them.

YOUR INNER WORLD: A DEEPER DIVE

Noticing your inner world can fuel incredibly intimate conversations. Here's how to practice noticing.

Feelings: Sometimes if we don't like an emotion, we choose to not pay attention to it. But emotions are present whether we pay attention to them or not. Awareness of your feelings can create massive shifts in your intimacy.

Thoughts: We all have at least one voice in our heads. Now: if you read that sentence and thought, "What voice? I don't have a voice in my head"—*that's* the voice. Thoughts can turn back into feelings when you notice them.

Judge/Saboteurs: Coined by Shirzad Chamine, 'Judge' and 'saboteurs' explain why we interpret life the way we do. Knowing yours can help you understand and accept yourself. Learn more at positiveintelligence.com

Reactions: Life happens and we react. But by bringing your reactions to your conscious awareness, you can free yourself from the cycle of becoming them. When you feel the instinct to react, just breathe and observe it.

Resentments form when our needs go unmet or our truths remain unspoken. In virtually every relationship, resentments cause separation. For now, just become aware of them. We'll explore how to express them in the next level.

Stories in your head vs. Intuition: The mind is designed to keep us safe. Ironically, we already have a mechanism for that: intuition. The mind looks for dangerous patterns. Intuition simply senses. There's more about this distinction on the next page.

Meanings: We assign meaning to others' words, actions or inactions based on assumptions. Notice and question your assumptions: what's my evidence? Could other interpretations exist? This awareness reduces miscommunication.

Wants/Needs: As toddlers, we cry to get what we want. As adults, we have to *ask* for what we want. And in the past, what we wanted may not always have mattered to others. Being aware of our wants and needs allows us to get them met.

HERE'S THE KEY TO NOTICING: WHATEVER YOU NOTICE IS OKAY. INTRUSIVE THOUGHTS, EMBARRASSING DESIRES, UNCOMFORTABLE EMOTIONS—THEY'RE NOT BAD OR WRONG. THEY JUST ARE. SO WHEN YOU NOTICE, NOTICE WITHOUT JUDGEMENT. AND IF YOU CAN'T, NOTICE THAT YOU'RE JUDGING YOURSELF AND MAKE THAT OKAY.

Have you ever interpreted a situation as something it wasn't? In Truth Empowered Relationships, we call that 'believing a story in your head.'

Our brains are wired to look for patterns and explanations, even when actual evidence is thin or nonexistent. It's a survival mechanism: the DMN helped our ancestors anticipate threats. But today, the DMN often fills in gaps in our perception with stories—shaped by **cognitive biases**, which make us see patterns that don't exist, and **confirmation biases**, which focus us only on evidence that fits our story while dismissing anything that contradicts it.

Translation: you may believe you've spotted a meaningful pattern in your partner's behavior, but what you perceive as 'meaning' might actually be coincidental, unrelated, even irrelevant.

A classic example is the film *The Damned United*. When a rival coach fails to shake young football manager Brian Clough's hand, he interprets it as a deliberate snub. The perceived slight fuels Clough's obsessive drive to surpass his rival. The reality? The rival coach *never saw Clough stick out his hand*. Yet Clough's belief in his story consumes him for years.

The key to overcoming the stories we tell ourselves is to challenge them. Question the evidence. Ask:

- Do I have proof, or am I relying on assumptions?
- Where is this belief coming from?
- What are the facts?
- What if I'm misperceiving things?

Questioning our stories lets us dismantle mental traps that lead to unnecessary conflict and suffering. We also strengthen our **metacognition**—the ability to think about our own thinking—which helps us recognize and reframe unhelpful narratives. And we sharpen our ability to tell when true intuition, rather than bias, is guiding us.

What story in your head might be shaping your perception of your partner? If you replaced it with curiosity, how might your relationship change?

BELIEVING A *Story* IN YOUR HEAD

HOW OUR MINDS CAN TRICK US

OWNING YOUR *Stream:*
THE POWER OF EMOTIONAL RESPONSIBILITY

In relationships, it's perhaps the single most transformative realization you can make: **you are responsible for your own emotional experience**. Your feelings come from within. No one can 'make' you feel something, just as you can't force emotions onto others. This concept is essential to a Truth Empowered Relationship.

When you take ownership of your emotions, you free yourself from the blame and projection that can wear down trust and intimacy. Consider how often we hear (or say!) things like, "You made me so angry!" or "You hurt me when you did that." While our emotions in those moments are real and valid, **blaming someone else for them isn't.** The feelings themselves come from our nervous systems, which are affected by our past, our triggers, our unique experiences and perceptions.

Imagine I ask you to "pass the milk." For most people, that's a completely neutral request. But my aunt associates that phrase with a painful memory. So if she hears it, she starts shaking inside. Is her reaction my fault? No. The reality is, others' reactions are shaped by experiences **we often know nothing about**. Her response is tied to her own history, not to my words.

The truth is, we all carry our own emotional worlds, full of layers others can't see. That means every trigger we experience is an opportunity, a chance to release stored emotional energy. That lets us reset, and experience the present free of emotional imprints from the past.

THE TRAP OF CODEPENDENCY
Relying on someone else to make you feel okay pulls you into the complicated dynamic of **codependency**. Instead of letting each person live their truth, codependency creates a pattern where one partner feels responsible for what the other feels. Emotions and self-worth get so tangled up that neither person can truly be themselves or stand on their own.

Codependency is draining, destabilizing and corrosive to the soul. It halts personal growth and prevents real healing. To short-circuit this pattern, a Truth Empowered Relationship cultivates emotional independence.

EMOTIONS: PERFECT AS THEY ARE
Emotions are messages from within, offering insight into our needs, boundaries and desires. They don't need 'fixing' because they're not flaws—they're signals, guiding us toward deeper self-understanding and growth.

In a Truth Empowered Relationship, when your partner feels uncomfortable, your role isn't to 'make them feel better.' It's to **hold space for them to experience and process their emotions**. The idea is to depend on ourselves for our sense of worth, not others. So release yourself from the burden of repairing your partner's emotional world. Just experience your truth and allow them to experience theirs.

What emotions do you judge, criticize or 'fix?'

Throughout history, humans have relied on noticing as a survival skill, reading the subtle cues in their environments and inner worlds to stay safe. Today, this skill can help us navigate the complexities of intimate relationships.

If you're not used to tuning in, noticing can be uncomfortable at first. You might see emotions you'd rather avoid, and patterns you're reluctant to face. But growth comes through discomfort. Every moment of noticing brings you closer to emotional freedom.

Here are tips to help strengthen your noticing muscle:

- Try micro-moments of noticing: tell your partner you might need ten seconds before you respond to them. Use this pause to notice and make sense of your internal reactions.
- Notice sensations in your body. Their wisdom speaks in ways other than words. For five minutes a day, scan for tension —tight shoulders, clenched jaw, fluttering chest—or ease. Then reflect on how these sensations might relate to your emotions.
- Approach your inner world like an explorer. Get curious about what you find: "Why is this emotion here? What might it be trying to tell me?" Judgment divides; curiosity connects..
- Noticing is just the first step; reflecting helps you make sense of it all. Reflecting takes you beyond noticing—you translate your inner world into insights you can act on.

We tend to move through life on autopilot: snapping at someone without really knowing why, or feeling upset without fully knowing where it's coming from.

But when you start noticing what's happening inside, you interrupt those automatic patterns, and replace them with clarity. This shift can dramatically improve how you communicate and resolve conflicts in your relationships.

Practical tips to help you

notice

WRITE DOWN WHAT YOU NOTICE

As you practice noticing, jotting down your observations will strengthen your connections with yourself and with your partner. Writing things down engages more areas of your brain than just thinking or talking about them; it stimulates the brain's **reticular activating system** (RAS), helping you focus on what matters most while it sharpens your self-awareness and memory. Plus, by giving words to your feelings and observations, you're better able to process and make sense of them. Think of it as planting seeds in the garden of your mind: each note you write down is a tiny act of creation, allowing the hidden patterns of your inner world to bloom into clarity—and enrich your conversations.

EXPLORE WHAT YOU NOTICE

Whatever you notice is okay—really. And if it catches your attention, there's a reason. So why not wonder about the why? Follow your curiosity about what you notice. By asking why, you open yourself up to a world of possibilities. Curiosity also strengthens neural connections, improving memory retention and problem-solving skills. It's no wonder many traditions see curiosity as a gateway to growth, and to rediscovering life's mystery and wonder. So welcome all your questions—even the unexpected ones, and the ones you judge. Your answers might surprise you— and maybe reshape how you see yourself and the world around you.

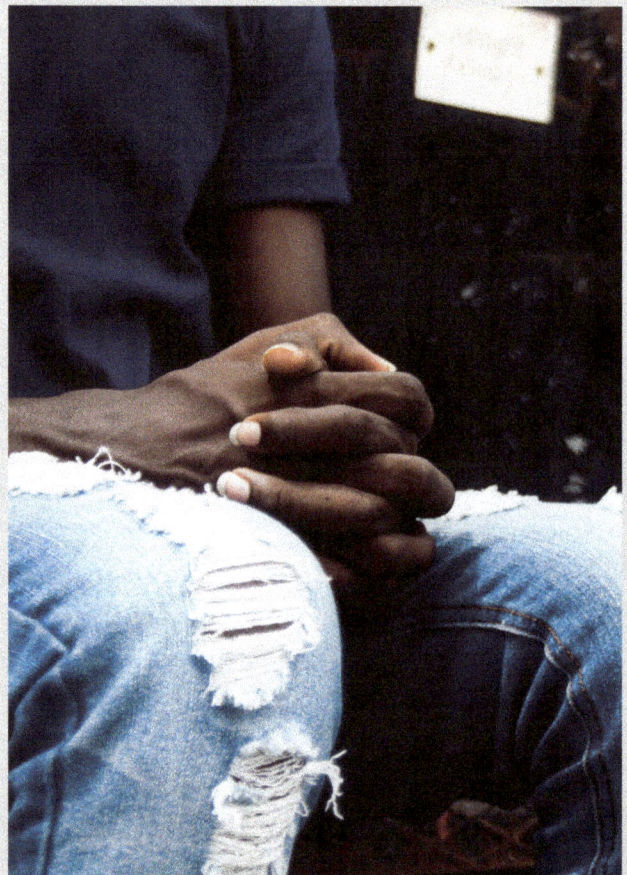

QUESTIONS THAT PROMPT YOU TO
Notice

Contemplate each prompt and journal what you notice.

Who are you comfortable talking about your feelings with? Why?

What's your definition of happiness?

In what ways are you preventing your own happiness?

How often do you treat yourself with love and respect? In what ways do you do it?

When you can't sleep at night, what thoughts tend to surface?

What inner reactions do you have when you see yourself in the mirror?

If you could get clear answers to three life questions, what would they be?

If you had to describe yourself in one sentence, what would it say?

What past challenges are you most proud of overcoming, and why?

What mistake taught you the most? What did you learn?

What advice would you give your teenage self, and why?

Which accomplishments are you most proud of, and why?

If success were guaranteed, what's the one thing you'd pursue?

If you could give yourself one meaningful message today, what would it be?

it's time to play

SEVEN NIGHTS OF TRUTH

Where you <u>practice noticing</u> your inner world

SEVEN NIGHTS OF TRUTH

FOR 1-2 PLAYERS

SUGGESTED LENGTH 5 MINUTES

OBJECT OF THE GAME

Cultivate self-awareness with your partner, through a shared, private reflection. Build the noticing muscle that will allow you to have Truth Empowered Convos.

HOW TO PLAY

Each night for seven nights, before bed, play Rock Paper Scissors. Winner goes first; the other person holds and marks the checklist on page 40.

Review the eight noticing categories on the checklist. For each category, each of you will:

- Contemplate the category silently for 30 seconds
- Notice what arises
- Add your check marks for that category, or nod to your partner to add it for you.

No need to discuss your discoveries yet. You'll learn to express them in Level 03, listen in Level 04, and have a Truth Empowered Convo in Level 05.

After your seven nights of truth, **advance to Level 03**.

A NOTE ON *Red Flags*

Remember a telltale sign in a particular relationship that you knew meant trouble, but you ignored it, talked yourself out of it, pushed it down? We can split ourselves in two wanting relationships to work.

If we invalidate our intuition long enough and intently enough, the cost is connection with ourselves. We settle for what we really don't want, because we don't tell the truth to ourselves, let alone our partner.

The Pillars of Truth Empowered Relationships are derived from clinical ethics. Its shared language harnesses elements of conscious communication, scientifically proven to deepen and strengthen intimacy. So if only one of you wants to commit to this method, it's highly likely you each want a different level of intimacy in your relationship.

Seven Nights of Truth requires just five minutes of contemplation. If you're unwilling to spend 300 seconds reflecting on your inner truth, I say you're resistant to looking inside. That's not bad or wrong. It's just a fact.

Someone who refuses to explore their truth will resist conscious communication. But a Truth Empowered Relationship *depends on* conscious communication. There is no lasting and deep emotional intimacy without it.

Agreeing to this method means agreeing to understand yourselves and each other, to express yourselves with clarity, sensitivity and respect—and to apologize, explain and reset when you fall short.

If that's not what you both want, that's okay. But I strongly suggest you view it as a red flag for your relationship—an indicator that your visions of intimacy don't align.

Use *Seven Nights of Truth* to see if real intimacy is for you. If you're reluctant, resistant or unwilling, take it seriously. Remove the rose-colored glasses and be honest about the level of intimacy you truly desire. Yes, Truth Empowered Relationships is a game...but it's only fun if you actually want to play.

WHEN YOU'RE WEARING ROSE-COLORED GLASSES, RED FLAGS JUST LOOK LIKE FLAGS.

SEVEN NIGHTS OF TRUTH

Start Date ....

Completion Date ....

Feelings	Thoughts	Judge and Saboteurs	Reactions	Resents	Stories / Intuition	Meanings	Wants / Needs
✓ ✓							

"Everything you'll ever need to know is within you;
the secrets of the universe are imprinted on the cells of your body."
— Dan Millman

LEVEL

03

LET'S DO IT!

**TRUTH EMPOWERED SPEAKING:
GIVING YOUR STREAM A VOICE** | 16 PAGES

What you will learn

You'll explore how to voice your inner world moment by moment, letting your words be shaped by the multifaceted truth of your stream. You'll be equipped with a structure and tools to express yourself with clarity, sensitivity, and respect, so you can bring the fullness of your unique authentic self to conversations.

"INTIMACY IS *allowing* THE OTHER TO SEE YOU AS YOU SEE *yourself.*"

—INSPIRED BY OSHO

Truth Empowered Speaking

THE UNDER

What's 'under the surface' for you about sharing. If you notice desires to avoid, suppress, resist or deny your share, begin by sharing those desires. End by sharing your *intention* for the convo—more on that later.

THE OVER

A movie trailer gives you an idea of what the movie's about without going into detail. Similarly, The Over is an overview of what you'll be talking about. it sets up the listener for what they're about to hear.

THE OUTER

The Outer is where you share your external observations. Describe them as neutrally as possible, without interpretation, to reduce the chance your listener takes them personally.

THE INNER

The Inner refers to your internal reactions to external events that we discussed in Level 02: your feelings, thoughts, saboteurs, impulses, meanings, resentments, stories and intuitions. (See pages 30-31 to refresh yourself on them.)

THE WHY

The Why is your reason for sharing—your deeper motivation. If your reason is 'altruism' or 'selflessness,' look deeper for your personal need or desire—your **selfish motivation**. More on this in Level 05.

THE ASK

The Ask is where you can make a request, based on what the experience helped you realize you want or need. After asking, say, "What did you notice about my request or what I shared?"

THE SWITCH

If you don't have a request, switch: ask, "What did you notice while you listened?" When they answer, just listen with grounded, neutral curiosity; we'll cover the structure of Truth Empowered Listening in the next level.

THE STRUCTURE

TRUTH EMPOWERED SPEAKING: PUTTING *you* INTO WORDS

It's time to begin putting your stream into words. We want your words to get accepted and understood. So before you talk, let's talk.

Your **stream** is the expression of your perspective on life. Streams work much like the channels of a TV. Just as you can change channels from a comedy to a thriller, when we go from relaxed to stressed, the way we experience life can be very different.

Putting your stream into words can cause your prefrontal cortex to suppress the brain area that produces emotional distress. Translation: **verbalizing your emotional pain can reduce your emotional pain.** Or said differently, being intimate about your inner world is scientifically proven to enhance your sense of well-being.

Seven Nights of Truth has been preparing you for this new level of intimacy. Remember *The Karate Kid?* The hero didn't realize while they were doing menial chores, they were also learning karate.

In the same way, *Seven Nights of Truth* has quietly built your noticing muscle—the key tool of a Truth Empowered Convo. Simply put, being able to notice will maximize your ability to intimately communicate your inner world.

(BTW, if you haven't completed *Seven Nights of Truth*, pause here and finish it first. Ask any pro athlete: mastery requires practice. Thanks to neuroplasticity, even five minutes a night can strengthen the neural pathways for self-awareness. For the sake of your relationship, find or make the time to practice.)

Two helpful tips before we go on:

- **I notice:** When you share your inner world, consider beginning each new awareness with *I notice*: "I notice I'm feeling sad" or "I notice my judge saying 'this is stupid.'" This creates **cognitive distancing**: when you don't associate yourself with what you observe, the observation becomes less likely to trigger you or your partner.
- **Keep returning to truth**: Being authentic can be challenging at first. You might feel the impulse to give up. If you do, simply name it: "I notice the impulse to give up." If you judge your words, say, "I notice myself judging my words." **Keep noticing and voicing what's true in each moment.**

OKAY. LET'S DEVELOP YOUR VOICE, AND MAKE SURE YOUR WORDS ARE A TRUE REFLECTION OF WHO YOU ARE. WE'LL START WITH WHAT WE KEEP HIDDEN.

Dropping the waterline

What sank the Titanic wasn't the 10 percent of the iceberg above the surface. It was the 90 percent *below* the surface.

Just as the Titanic was undone by the vast portion of the iceberg lurking beneath the water, the things we keep buried in our hearts—our hidden fears, unmet needs, unspoken thoughts—can quietly sink a relationship if they're left unaddressed.

In a Truth Empowered Relationship, dropping the waterline means embracing radical transparency—bringing to light the truths we often keep submerged. This method asks you as partners to share the fears, insecurities, traumas and longings you assume might push your partner away. Ironically, sharing these truths doesn't erode connection—it's keeping them hidden that does it.

When you both bring everything to the surface, you can address issues before they become emotional icebergs. Your relationship goes from avoiding hidden dangers to floating calmly on the crystal-clear waters of openness and trust.

Dropping the waterline doesn't mean endlessly airing complaints or grievances. It simply asks you to create the habit of sharing your truth in the moment—especially if it's a resentment. That way, nothing stays hidden long enough to damage your connection. Bring your ice into the light—and watch it be melted by the healing power of intimacy.

Where in your relationship can you drop the waterline?

TRUTH EMPOWERED SPEAKING:
Tips for the speaker

The conscious communication techniques of Truth Empowered Speaking can transform relationships. They help you share precise, unbiased, emotionally responsible information, reducing your chances of misunderstandings and conflict. They also boost your **emotional intelligence (EQ)**—meaning you'll be able to navigate your and others' emotions more easily.

Along the way, you'll uncover motivations, spark meaningful dialogues, and gain deeper insights.

TRUTH GIVES THE REAL YOU A CHANCE TO BE SEEN, UNDERSTOOD AND LOVED.

Remember: **practice makes progress**, just like learning any language. Start with smaller, less charged discussions to build confidence. As you grow comfortable, apply these techniques to daily talks, and then more complex discussions.

Mastering these steps is an ongoing journey. Every convo is an opportunity to refine your skills and build a more meaningful connection.

• **Schedule time:** Truth Empowered Convos take presence and focus. Set aside 15 minutes. If the convo's not over, agree to extend or reschedule.

• **Struggling to identify your thoughts?** *Tell your partner,* 'I can't identify my thoughts.' For help uncovering some of the 'voices' influencing your stream, visit positiveintelligence.com

• **Can't identify your feelings or needs?** *Say so.* Then visit cnvc.org. Also try journaling: it grows your ability to tune into your inner state.

• **Feeling resistant?** *Name it:* 'I'm worried about being judged,' or 'I'm scared to hurt your feelings.' Then use 'The Why' step to uncover the deeper reasons behind your resistance.

• **Overwhelmed?** *Say it,* then regulate with slow, deep breaths while you wiggle your toes.

• **Not aware of having feelings?** As we talked about earlier, when we're tuned out of our feelings, our psyche starts calling them 'tension.' Can you find your tension?

• **Challenges remaining neutral in The Outer?** Neutrality isn't suppressing your perspective. It's presenting observations in an emotionally responsible way that minimizes blame.

• **Can't find the right words?** Try metaphors or descriptive language. Describing the opposite of what you feel can also provide clarity.

TRUTH EMPOWERED SPEAKING:
The listener's role

Level 04 centers on mastering the art of listening—a skill that transforms conversations and relationships. In this level, as the listener, your role is simple: **be fully present.** Focus on receiving, not responding.

Imagine yourself as a witness to the speaker's experience, a safe harbor for their inner world. Your grounded presence creates the stability they need to explore and process their truth.

TRUTH HONORS WHO YOU ARE;
LISTENING HONORS TRUTH.

Buddhist and Native American traditions see listening without judgment as a profound gift: it honors the speaker's experience without imposing the listener's ego or interpretations, and supports the speaker in self-reflection and in releasing emotions.

This kind of listening gives the speaker something rare: the freedom to let their words flow naturally, without fear of being interrupted or judged. That invites deeper vulnerability—and leads to deeper understanding.

- Listen with your full attention: put away distractions like your phone. Also, nonverbal cues, like an engaged posture and uncrossed arms, show your presence and respect.

- If you find the speaker's flow hard to follow, that's okay: just let their words wash over you, and trust that your time and presence will lead to understanding.

- When distracting thoughts, judgments, or the urge to offer advice creep in, simply notice and acknowledge the impulse, and guide your attention back to the speaker.

- If you lose focus, ground yourself with slow, deep breaths; then silently and neutrally summarize what you're hearing: "They're sharing their feelings."

- If you're tracking with the speaker, you can acknowledge it with simple nods or a soft 'mmm,' but avoid interrupting their flow.

- When the speaker's done, don't comment or solve. Say "I heard you." If they made a request, acknowledge it without acting on it right away by saying "I heard your request."

- You can also ask **CQs: Clarifying Questions** (if you're confused) and **Curious Questions** (if you're curious). Make sure they don't contain hidden judgments or advice.

Validating intuition:
THE SCIENCE OF TELLING THE TRUTH
WHEN YOU'VE BEEN LYING

Our brains are wired to spot patterns, on a never-ending search for consistency. When something feels off—like when we sense someone's being dishonest with us—it triggers **cognitive dissonance:** our intuition clashing with what we're being told. That activates the **anterior cingulate cortex**, our brain's error detector—to resolve the conflict. The process creates tension and anxiety, much like a crooked picture frame on a wall—we can't stop noticing it, and we can't relax until it's straight.

Here's the flip side: truth-telling calms the brain. When our gut feeling lines up with what's said, we're no longer trying to reconcile conflicting information, so the static clears and stress fades. The listener's amygdala quiets, allowing their brain to shift from conflict to connection. We feel relief: that crooked frame's now aligned.

Ever told your partner you're fine when you're not? They often sense something's off, even if they can't pinpoint it, creating tension for you both. But share the truth—"I'm upset because I felt unheard earlier"—and you replace confusion with clarity, opening the door to connection.

In a Truth Empowered Relationship, honoring your partner means validating their intuition, even when it's hard. You'll ease their self-doubt, because they'll know their feelings are justified. And since dishonesty can make anyone second-guess themselves, your truth could even boost their confidence. So choose truth. You'll nurture their trust in you—and their belief in themselves.

Where in your relationship could sharing your truth bring clarity instead of confusion?

"This feels awkward."
STAYING WITH THE PROCESS

Expressing yourself in this new way can feel awkward. Stay with it. Like learning any new language, you start with a limited vocabulary, stumbling as you put words together.

When you feel like running, hiding or cringing, *say it*. Sharing The Under—**speaking your resistance**—helps disarm the resistance.

I also suggested you use "I notice" to create cognitive distancing, which separates what you observe from who you are. If "I notice" feels robotic, get creative with your phrasing:

- *"I observed* my judge…"
- *"I felt* the impulse…"
- *"I'm witnessing* a story in my head…"
- *"I'm hearing* a saboteur say…"
- *"I saw* the meaning I gave…"
- *"I sensed* a reaction to…"
- *"I'm aware* of a resentment…"

Sharing vulnerably can trigger discomfort, as your brain fears rejection. You might feel tempted to cut yourself off by saying "never mind" or "it doesn't matter." Resist that urge —share anyway.

Why? Expressing yourself honestly boosts dopamine and enhances self-worth. And each time you speak your truth, you retrain your nervous system to link honesty with connection, reshaping how your brain views vulnerability. It's like turning a locked door into an open one.

Truth Empowered Speaking builds new **neuronal pathways** for authentic communicating. Practicing daily strengthens these pathways—and within about 30 days, they become automatic. Your nervous system will be rewired for emotional authenticity—which leads to deeper intimacy.

TRUTH EMPOWERED SPEAKING:
Frequently asked questions

WHY DO WE SHARE THE UNDER?

Most of us have a fear-driven voice inside that tells us not to speak our truth. To disable this resistance, speak to it: state why you don't want to say what you're about to say. Then…say it anyway. You'll be amazed how much easier saying what you don't want to say becomes.

WHAT IF I DON'T KNOW HOW TO START?

Speak to that resistance: "I don't know how to start." Not sure what to say next? "I'm not sure what to say next." Worried about every word you say? "I'm worried about every word I say." Not sure what you need? "I'm not sure what I need." Vocalize what's stopping you.

WHY DOES THE OUTER NEED TO BE NEUTRAL?

Using neutral language for The Outer helps prevent misunderstandings and conflicts. When you describe actions factually ("You left the room"), versus subjectively ("You abandoned me"), you reduce the likelihood of defensiveness or arguments about what happened. Neutrality keeps convos from derailing.

CAN YOU GIVE AN EXAMPLE OF A SHARE?

"When you left the room, I saw I felt anxious. I noticed the thought 'He hates me.' I witnessed my judge and perfectionist calling me silly. I felt the impulse to pull my hair. I realize I resented you for not talking. I made up a story in my head that you were mad at me. And I recognized I made your leaving mean I'm unlovable."

WHAT IF WHAT I SHARE MAKES ME LOOK BAD?

In our actions and words, there's always that selfish motivation I mentioned earlier. Maybe we want a feeling we enjoy. Maybe we want to get love, or not lose love. Counterintuitive as it sounds, admitting a motivation you believe makes you look 'bad' makes you in fact look *honest*. That builds closeness and trust. Again, we'll discuss selfish motivations more in Level 05.

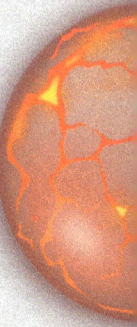

Noticing your own state of elevation demonstrates emotional mastery and advanced self-awareness. Neuroscience tells us this awareness plays a critical role in managing stress and in navigating your interactions with others.

In our next game, *Boiling Point*, you'll practice noticing when you're elevated. The secret is to notice when you're feeling something in the **anger spectrum**, like frustration, irritation, impatience or annoyance. Anger is often a secondary emotion, masking feelings like overwhelm or helplessness—that might be signaling a need for support we're resisting or ignoring. Noticing these moments is key for having thriving relationships.

To shift your state when you're elevated, try this powerful hack: name your anger emotion as soon as you recognize it. Simply saying "I'm angry" acts as a neurological reset, engaging the prefrontal cortex to regulate the amygdala, the brain's fear center. This reduces the stress response, helping you transition from reactive to calm.

Unsure why you feel elevated? Ask, "Why *might* I be feeling this way?" Adding 'might' primes your brain for insight even if you don't land on an immediate answer. Staying curious creates space for understanding, and helps recalibrate your emotional state.

Getting *elevated*

it's time to play

BOILING POINT

Where you notice your inner world when you're angry

BOILING POINT

OBJECT OF THE GAME

Develop self-awareness by tuning into your inner world during moments of heightened emotion. Practice consciously communicating your stream, even in the midst of intense feelings.

HOW TO PLAY

For three days, notice whenever you feel an emotion in the anger spectrum—like irritation, frustration, impatience or annoyance.

Every time you notice, look also for **thoughts, meanings, resentments, stories or intuition,** and **wants or needs**. And ask *why* you're feeling this way, *when* you've felt this feeling before, and *what* the feeling reminds you of. Get to know these parts of your inner world. The next two pages explain why this matters to your relationship.

In addition, if you're speaking during the experience, notice if your voice gets louder, higher, faster, or if your energy feels more intense. That's a sign you're getting elevated. Noticing when we're elevated keeps a Truth Empowered Conversation safe. If you do notice, say simply "I notice I'm getting elevated. I'm feeling [angry]" (name the anger-spectrum emotion you're feeling).

Practice this for three days, then advance to Level 04.

A NOTE ON
Meanings...

Why does the same event make one person laugh and another one rage? Often, it's not the event itself but the meaning we attach to it that shapes our reaction.

Our brains are storytelling machines, constantly interpreting the world through the lens of our past. At the first hint of conflict or uncertainty, the brain's emotional command center, our **limbic system**, leaps into action, instantly assigning meaning based on our memories, experiences, and unconscious beliefs. It's your brain's way of keeping you safe—but it's not always accurate. That's why an offhand comment might feel like a personal attack, or a forgotten text can seem like proof of rejection.

To break this cycle, we need to move from the limbic system's knee-jerk reaction to the prefrontal cortex's reasoning and reflection This means catching yourself in the act of reacting, and instead finding out what meaning you've given to the situation.

Naming emotions is a powerful first step: saying "I'm angry" instead of getting angry. From there, dig deeper: *"Where is this feeling coming from? What's the root?"* Identifying the roots lets you find whatever meaning you've attached, and question whether it's serving you—or holding you back.

Our brains rely on **pattern recognition** —mental shortcuts that draw on past experiences to interpret the present. The problem? The patterns we believe we perceive aren't always real. But unpacking the meaning behind our emotions shifts us from automatic reacting to thoughtful reflecting.

So explore these layers. Find out what your meanings are, and where they're coming from.

Reflect on what triggered your anger during Boiling Point. *Did your anger reveal an old wound or unmet need? What's your story about the anger? Can you separate the event itself from the meaning you attached to it? Could another perspective exist?*

...AND HOW THEY CONNECT TO *Timelines*

When you meet someone and fall in love, it's easy to think your shared story is all that matters. But each of you entered the relationship with your own timeline—a unique path stretching back to the moment you entered this world.

Long before you met, your timeline was shaping you. Every high and low, every belief you formed, every meaning you attached to your experiences left its mark. The same's true for your partner. When you come together, you're not just connecting in the present. You're also merging years of history—most of it unknown to each other.

That's why exploring each other's timelines is so essential. Behind many of your partner's reactions, habits or sensitive spots are stories tied to moments you weren't there to witness. It could be an early memory of rejection, a pivotal friendship, or a hard-earned life lesson. Delving into these chapters helps you discover the meanings your partner gives to things, and understand why they are the way they are. This strengthens the brain's empathy circuits—replacing conflict with compassion.

Many cultures believe you must know someone's entire journey to appreciate their true self. Psychologically, that understanding creates what's called **earned secure attachment**—a feeling of being deeply known and accepted by your partner. When you honor the timelines that shaped each other, you open the door to a more profound connection.

What story from your timeline might help your partner 'get you?'

LEVEL

04

TRUTH EMPOWERED LISTENING;
HEARING BEYOND WORDS | 21 PAGES +
WORKSHEET

LET'S GO!

What you will learn

Let's tune into the nuances not just of what's said, but also what's unsaid and what's sensed. You'll learn to listen with your whole being, creating a sanctuary for sharing. You'll let curiosity and openness guide you in asking the thoughtful questions that enrich intimacy. You'll enhance your ability to understand your partner.

"THE MOST BASIC OF ALL HUMAN NEEDS IS TO *understand* AND BE *understood.*

THE BEST WAY TO UNDERSTAND PEOPLE IS TO *listen* TO THEM."

—RALPH G. NICHOLS

THE QUESTIONS

While you listen, you might notice *Clarifying Questions* (when you're confused) and *Curious Questions* (things you wonder about). In that order, start your Report with these CQs.

THE WORDS

As you listen to The Words, remember: **ABC— Always Be Curious**. Imagine you're the host of a podcast or talk show, wanting to uncover not just the details of your guest's story, but also its dimensionality.

THE INNER

The Inner is what's happening inside you as you listen. Notice the elements of your inner world we discussed on pages 30-31, while you maintain focus on what's being said.

THE OUTER

The Outer is the speaker's body language, facial expressions, gestures—the things that can be observed with the eyes. Often, observing these will reveal emotions or truths that their words don't fully convey.

THE UNDERCURRENTS

The Undercurrents are the subtleties in the speaker's tone and intensity. Do their words align with their energy, or are there unspoken emotions woven beneath them?

REPORT AND RESPOND

When the speaker finishes, start with a **report**: ask CQs, then summarize The Words and adjust if needed. Next, **respond**: share your Inner, Outer and Undercurrents. If they made a request, reply with your inner truth about it.

THE SWITCH

Then it's time again for the switch. Speaker: did the listener seem to understand your experience? What were your reactions to their response?

TRUTH EMPOWERED LISTENING: THE ART OF *shifting perspectives*

True listening is about experiencing the world through someone else's point of view. It's a skill most of us tap into when we watch movies or shows. We experience our version of the main character's journey: their triumphs, their tragedies—and their inner world about it all.

That's what happens in conversations when we listen deeply: **we step out of our own perspective and into the speaker's viewpoint**, which may be very different than our own.

Being able to shift perspectives enhances conversations: you don't just understand what someone says—you get how they experienced it. Immersing yourself in their point of view also gives you easier access to empathy, and reduces misunderstandings.

And just like each movie is different, each person's perspective is unique. Listening that toggles between your viewpoint and theirs creates a bridge of connection where real understanding can flow.

At our son's middle-school orientation, the orchestra teacher said students had to practice Monday through Friday. Some parents groaned. The teacher added, "I used to make them practice seven days a week...then *I* had kids."

Perspective shift. The parents laughed, feeling understood.

When you're open to your perspectives shifting, you're open to really getting to know someone. Perspective shifts don't mean you have to adopt the new perspective—just understand it.

A listening mastery hack: **find the fascination in their story, or in their telling of it**. That makes listening an act of exploration, of discovery.

None of us has the master plan to life, though we may believe we do. Seeing through another's eyes can expand your own vision of life too.

Seek to understand:
CHANGING YOUR FOCUS IN CONVERSATIONS

Seeking to understand isn't just about understanding your partner. It's also about understanding yourself. So in Truth Empowered Speaking, the listener is checking their inner world during a conversation too. *What's my truth? What am I feeling?*

You're also listening beyond words, tuning into what's beneath the surface: the speaker's tone, their pauses, the emotions behind their words. Instead of thinking, "Why are they being difficult?" you ask, "What might they be feeling or needing right now?"

Studies show reflecting on our inner experience during conversations increases our openness, and builds our resilience for when conflict arises. Plus, when we feel understood, our brains produce less **cortisol**, the stress hormone, and more **oxytocin**, the 'love hormone.' Oxytocin calms anxiety and fosters trust, so we're more able to open up.

So what unlocks understanding? Curiosity. It fuels **cognitive flexibility**: the ability to shift perspectives and consider multiple truths. Cognitive flexibility can turn defensiveness into connectedness.

Curiosity also keeps the amygdala's alarms from overreacting, and allows the perspective-taking prefrontal cortex to stay in charge. This makes it easier to understand feelings—ours and theirs—and fills conversations with calm and depth.

So ABC: Always Be Curious. Start with youself: explore your feelings and intentions. Then bring that same curiosity to your partner. Curiosity as a mindset transforms communicating into understanding. When you both 'get' yourselves and each other, truth flows more freely, and intimacy becomes second nature.

What Curious Question could you ask your partner?

Truth Empowered Listening:

Helpful hints

Write It Down:
Taking notes while you listen engages motor, language and visual areas of your brain—boosting memory and aiding in comprehension. It also creates stronger neural connections, so you'll recall the conversation more accurately later.

Pause Eye Contact For Notes:
Maintaining eye contact takes cognitive effort. Briefly breaking it to jot notes frees mental space for more effective processing.

Use a Gesture to Pause the Flow:
If the speaker is talking faster than you can jot down notes, raise your index finger—a polite request for a pause. This shows you value their words while making sure you don't miss key details. Lower your finger once you're caught up.

Paraphrase as You Write:
Restating in your own words what you listen to helps you process and take in what you heard. Known as active listening, this technique reinforces your understanding, and makes the speaker feel truly heard.

Validate with Nonverbal Cues While You Write:
Nods, smiles or brief eye contact while you jot your notes show you're still engaged, so you can maintain the connection while you juggle writing and listening.

When Something Feels Off:
If your intuition flags something as inconsistent, jot down a quick note: 'X doesn't align with Y—ask more later.' This acknowledges your inner alarm, but keeps it from derailing your attention, so you can stay curious while you let the full story reveal itself.

TRUTH EMPOWERED LISTENING:
Frequently asked questions

WHY DO I NEED TO NOTICE MY INNER REACTIONS?

Your inner reactions shape how you interpret the speaker's words. By noticing them, you create space to listen without letting those reactions filter or distort their message. You also lay the groundwork for sharing your inner world—*your* side of the intimate dialogue.

HOW DO I STAY NEUTRAL IF I HAVE REACTIONS?

Neutrality doesn't mean suppressing your reactions—it means allowing them without judgment. Whatever reactions you have are *okay*, so notice and let them be, without letting them disrupt your listening. When it's your turn, say "I notice I'm *feeling* triggered" instead of *getting* triggered.

WHAT IF I FEEL DEFENSIVE WHILE I LISTEN?

Defensiveness is natural, and noticing it is key. Stay present and curious about the speaker's message. When it's your turn, share your Inner as, "I see I felt defensive when you said…" Instead of *getting* defensive, share that you *feel* defensive. **Consciousness reduces conflicts**.

WHAT IF I DISAGREE WITH THE SPEAKER?

No two people have the same perspectives on every aspect of life. But Truth Empowered Listening isn't about agreeing—it's about understanding. Notice your differing viewpoint without losing focus on listening. When it's your turn, share as part of your Inner: "I notice my judge saying this about what you said."

WHAT IF I DON'T UNDERSTAND THE SPEAKER?

If you're confused or uncertain about what the speaker is saying, or if you notice a gap in their story, ask CQs at the start of your Report, before The Words. For example: "So what did she say back after you said that?" Or "Can you explain what you meant by this?"

Holding space *for silence*

Coming from a background where interrupting was common, I've seen how it does more than halt a conversation—it disrupts the flow of thought and emotion. When we interrupt, we potentially blow out the flame of someone's connection to their inner world.

The urge to interrupt—to defend or correct—can be surprisingly strong. But once we interrupt someone's stream, it may not return in the same way—or at all. The idea of 'if you forgot, it must not've been important' doesn't take into account that what someone's about to share often arises organically from the flow of the conversation. Interruptions stop the flow, which can cause those unspoken words to be lost.

Truth Empowered Listening holds space for silence. Embracing silence in a conversation invites transformation. Here's why.

By activating the speaker's DMN, the brain's introspection hub, silence gives the speaker the room they need to connect dots, uncover insights, and process emotions. It can be like sunlight breaking through a curtain: the amygdala quiets and the prefrontal cortex takes over, which gives rise to calm and thoughtful reflection. In silence, the speaker often finds the words they didn't even know they were searching for.

In mindfulness meditation, stillness is the mind's gateway to clarity. Eastern philosophies teach us that silence is not empty but full of possibility—a space where wisdom and self-awareness are born. Native American traditions consider silence sacred: they see it as a time to absorb and honor the speaker's journey.

If you feel the impulse to interrupt, take a breath to ground yourself, and remind yourself —as I do—that **preserving your partner's connection to their inner experience** is what matters most. Often, if you allow the conversation to continue uninterrupted, whatever response or point you wanted to share will resolve itself naturally.

Allowing silence tells your partner that you cherish their connection to their own voice. That changes not only what they share, but also the way they share it. The conversation deepens in unexpected ways—and every exchange holds the potential to bring you closer.

Listening when it's about *you* can heighten your emotions and cloud your understanding. Here's how to stay grounded and present.

The act of listening can be uniquely challenging when what's being said is about you. You may feel almost compelled to respond, like a reflex. Instead, jot down your reactions while silently acknowledging them: "I feel angry" or "I feel hurt." Not sure what you feel? Don't pause to examine it now; simply say to yourself, "I feel triggered."

Neurologically, writing down your feelings while you silently acknowledge them stops your attention from getting hijacked, moving you from reactive to reflective. And it doesn't stop the conversation or interrupt the speaker's flow. It simply gives you a moment to regulate, so you can stay present rather than being swept away by your emotions.

Biases—assumptions or opinions about what the speaker's saying or why—can pop up as well. To counteract this, adopt a mindset of "This is their truth, not mine." If you notice judgmental thoughts or interpretations, note them with neutrality and redirect your attention to the speaker's words.

And if you don't feel neutral about something, don't force neutrality. Instead, **be neutral about the fact that you aren't neutral.**

If you need extra help remaining present, ground yourself: take slow, intentional breaths; mentally repeat an affirmation like "Stay curious, not critical;" or gently press your feet into the floor.

Cognitive psychology tells us our brains want closure, to relieve anxiety. Trust the process. You'll have your turn to speak. Practicing patience keeps the conversation moving instead of spiraling.

CUE THE QUESTIONS

By noticing cues and asking the right questions, you can transform relationships and lives.

Trained therapists and coaches are skilled at spotting subtle cues in a conversation that signal opportunities for deeper understanding, and asking questions that can create transformational depth. With some practice, you can build that skill too.

Here's a guide to understanding some of these cues:

• **Deleted Info**: Glossing over or skipping key details in a conversation—with phrases like "we talked it out" or "then things got better"—can mean the speaker's leaving out important portions of what happened. Ask "How did you talk it out?" or "What made things better?"

• **Charged Info**: Putting extra emphasis or emotional weight on certain words or names is often a sign of hidden significance. So if they say, "I went with Kayla, Noah, *Ian*, and Amy," with extra emphasis on 'Ian,' you might ask, "I noticed you put emphasis on Ian. Is there a reason?"

• **Repeated Info**: Repeating the same fact or detail multiple times often signals its emotional or cognitive significance to the speaker. Ask, "You mentioned that a few times—what makes it so important to you?" This helps them explore why this detail reoccurs so frequently.

• **Triggering Info**: If the speaker suddenly goes quiet, shuts down, or becomes emotional after mentioning something, it's a sign that this topic holds deeper significance or pain. Ask "I noticed you went quiet there—what's coming up for you?" or "Is this part hard to talk about?"

• **Mismatched Info**: If something the speaker says doesn't quite align with what they've said before or with how they're acting, it may indicate conflicting feelings or internal struggles. So for example, if they say "I'm fine," while their body language and tone suggests otherwise, you might respond, "You say you're okay, but your body language and energy don't match your words. Is there more to share?"

THREADS: THE SEEDS OF FUTURE INTIMACY

While you engage with this conversation, you can also notice what the next one might be about.

Threads are topics that you might notice emerging during a conversation, but pursuing them in the moment would derail the conversation.

Threads are a conversation's hidden seeds: small, easily overlooked details that, when revisited, can grow into deeper understanding or open new avenues of discovery. They're often easy to miss, buried in the flow of their words as they speak, and of your inner stream as you listen. Yet these threads hold the potential for meaningful future conversations. A mention of a childhood memory, a passing reference to a major event, a subtle hint at an unresolved issue—these can lead to your next Truth Empowered Convo.

Recognizing Threads is an art in itself. As you cultivate your ability to listen with curiosity, you'll start to notice when something catches your attention or sparks your interest, but it doesn't quite fit the current conversation's flow. For example, if someone says, "...so I met her on Oak Street—first time I've been there since this weird thing happened five years ago. Anyway, she's crying because her boyfriend said..."

Now, you might well feel the urge to ask about the weird thing that happened. But since the topic at hand is something else entirely, pulling on that Thread could unravel the flow. Instead, let the speaker know that, while you listen, you keep track of things you notice while you're listening. Then preserve those Threads: jot them down as you listen, like bookmarking or dog-earing a page in a book that you want to return to later.

Notice Threads and your intimate dialogues will never run dry. In addition, therapists and coaches like me listen for Threads because unwinding them often leads to transformational insights. By listening for Threads in your relationship, you become a source of deep convos, and a catalyst for meaningful change in the life of this person who matters so much to you.

INTERMEDIATE

TALK SHOW

FOR 2 PLAYERS

SUGGESTED LENGTH
60 MINUTES

OBJECT OF THE GAME

To deepen connection and strengthen understanding by practicing conscious, truthful listening and speaking.

What do we enjoy about talk shows? The relatable stories, the engaged byplay. That's what "Talk Show" is designed to replicate.

HOW TO PLAY

*NOTE: Read the next seven pages before you play. If this game feels awkward at first, **stay with it**. Practice makes progress.*

Rock Paper Scissors: winner is Guest. **Set a timer** for one hour.

Guest, reflect on your responses on page 08 about limiting conversations, and on any shifts you've noticed since you wrote them. Then, using Truth Empowered Speaking (Under, Over, Inner, Outer, Why, Ask), express your inner world about them.

Host, listen with curiosity, without interrupting or fixing. Listen to understand. Notice both the words, and the emotions and nuances behind them. Write down your inner-world noticings and your CQs. Seek to uncover the Guest's deeper truth.

After Guest's done, Host makes sure they understand by giving their **report** (CQs plus Words); then they **respond** with Inner reactions, Outer observations, and Undercurrents noticed.

Host: After you respond, ask, **"Is there more for you?"** Continue until Guest says, 'No, is there more for you?' Then **switch roles** and repeat until you both answer 'no,' or until timer goes off.

Reflect on the experience with the prompts on page 82.

TRUTH EMPOWERED SPEAKING: *The Guest*

Guest, this is your moment to share something meaningful to you—a story, a withheld truth, a request. The more emotionally risky the share, the more likely it is that the share creates a shift in the depth of your intimacy.

GUEST TIPS

Feel Safe to Share: Express yourself openly and honestly. This setup's designed to be conflict-free, so you don't need to censor your feelings. This is your chance to speak your truth.

Ground Yourself in the Moment: Take a moment to settle in before you start sharing. Wiggle your toes. Take a slow, deep breath. Grounding can ease nervousness and bring you present. When you're present, you're more likely to stay connected to your inner truth as you share.

Let Go of the Need to Perform: When we're new at Truth Empowered Speaking, we might get caught up in saying things the right way, or the entertaining way. Remember, *Talk Show* is a practice, not a performance. Your words don't need to be perfect or witty—they just need to be real. Embrace sincerity over polish.

Flow from Your Inner World: Allow what you notice to form your words, even if they feel raw or incomplete. Explore as you speak. This is your chance to dig into and share your inner world and get seen and accepted for it.

It's Okay to Pause Mid-Share: If you're unsure where to go next, take a moment. Reflecting in real-time often leads to unexpected insights and deeper shares. The Host knows to hold space for silence, so sit in the stillness and let what's next emerge.

Embrace The Why: Sharing the reason you say what you say—also called *setting a context*—instantly gives the listener more understanding.

These practices will help make your shares more natural, fulfilling, and genuinely connecting.

TRUTH EMPOWERED LISTENING: *The Host*

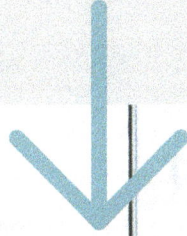

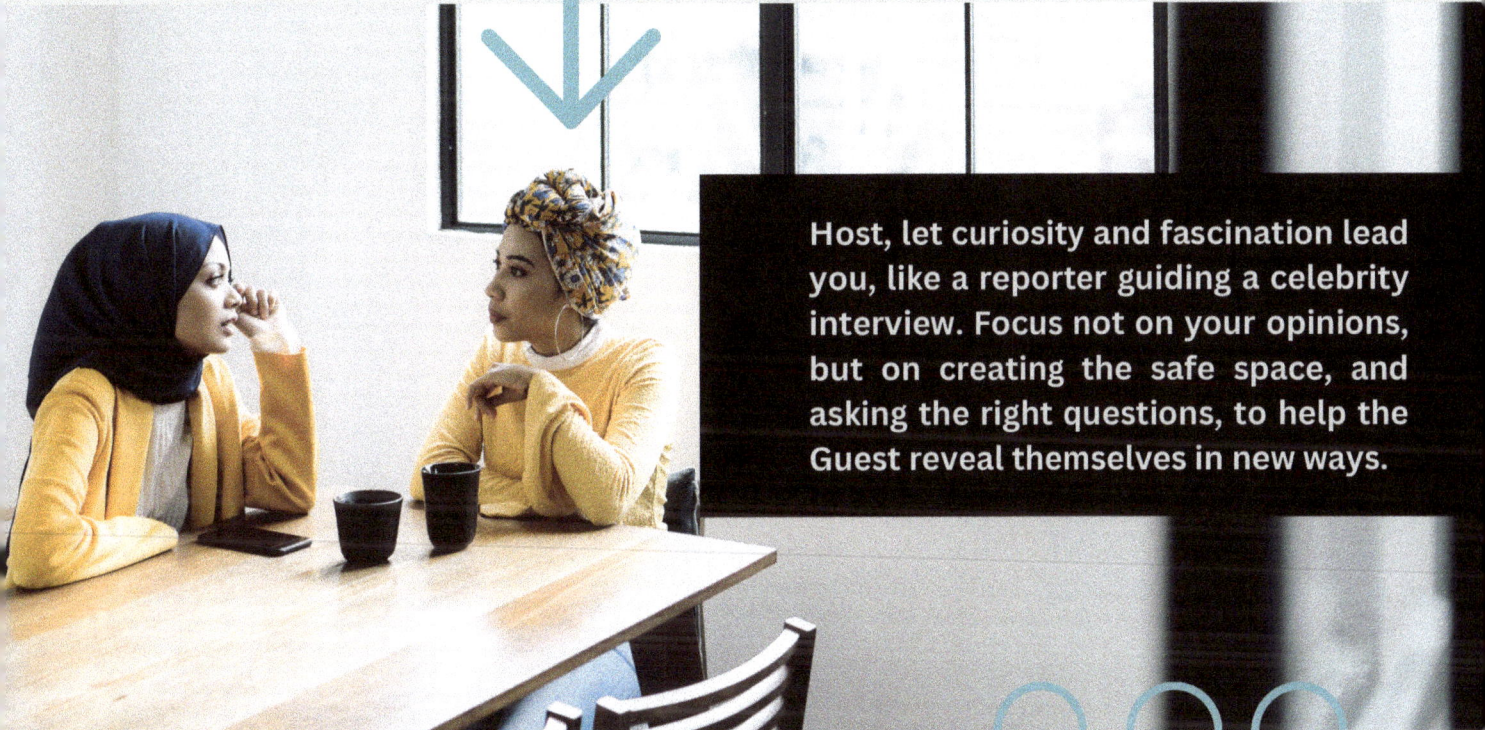

Host, let curiosity and fascination lead you, like a reporter guiding a celebrity interview. Focus not on your opinions, but on creating the safe space, and asking the right questions, to help the Guest reveal themselves in new ways.

HOST TIPS

Listen Beyond the Words: Listen beyond the Guest's words and content. Their pauses, tone, points of emphasis and word choices reveal the subtext of what they share—and what they may be holding back.

Be Responsible for Your Emotions and Reactions: As you listen, it's natural to have emotions, reactions, even judgments. Notice these, without letting them pull you away from the Guest's story. You'll get a chance to express them. For now, quietly acknowledge them, and stay grounded. Focus on creating a safe and non-judgmental environment for the Guest.

Let Go of Preconceived Notions: Assume you know nothing about the Guest's story—even if you've heard it already. This mindset opens you up to nuances you might've otherwise missed, and to new info the Guest might reveal.

Ask Depth-Charged Questions: These questions naturally expand the Guest's story. For example, if they mention feeling nervous, ask "What was the nervousness about?" Questions like these can spark deeper insights, that help the Guest see and share their story in a new way.

Let Curiosity Guide You Back: If you're distracted as you listen, note it so you can explore it later, and refocus on the Guest by fueling your curiosity: "What interests me in their story? What might they be glossing over, and why? Why did they emphasize that word? What do I sense behind their words? What can I ask to help them reflect more deeply?"

To **Report and Respond**, a) ask CQs; b) give a neutral summary of The Words; c) share Inner, Outer and Undercurrents; d) acknowledge any request by sharing your Inner response to it.

76

Truth Empowered Speaking.

Chris and Taylor, a married couple, are feeling tension over a recurring issue: Chris often works late, leaving Taylor alone at home with their young child. Taylor's tried to bring it up before, but it often leads to defensiveness and unresolved frustration. Today, Taylor decides to approach the conversation with Truth Empowered Speaking, as the Guest on "Talk Show."

The Under:

- Avoiding this convo because I'm scared Chris will feel blamed.
- Judge: "Chris won't change-it's just who they are."
- Reaction: Want to stay calm; fear I'll snap instead.
- Intention: to care about <u>both</u> of our feelings and needs (don't forget to say that!)

The Over:

I need to talk about not feeling supported when Chris works late.

The Outer:

- Chris worked late every night this week.
- Didn't tell me beforehand.
- Left me to handle everything at home alone: dinner, homework, bedtime.

The Inner:

- Feelings: Overwhelmed, lonely, hurt, a little resentful.
- Thoughts: "Why don't they realize how hard this is for me?"
- Meaning: I'm carrying more than my share of responsibility.
- Story: Chris doesn't care or notice how much I'm struggling.
- Saboteurs: My Judge says they should already know this.

The Why:

- I want to feel like we're a team, not like I'm on my own.
- Need: Better communication and shared responsibilities.

The Ask:

- Can you communicate earlier when you'll be late?
- Can we plan a way to share evening tasks better?

GUEST'S SAMPLE SHARE

"Chris, I've been avoiding bringing this up because I'm afraid it will come across like I'm blaming you, so I want you to know: my intention is to care about your feelings and needs, while I also care about mine.

This week, you worked late every night, and you didn't let me know ahead of time. That left me managing dinner, helping Avery with homework, and getting them to bed on my own. I noticed myself feeling overwhelmed, lonely, hurt, and even a bit resentful.

I see this story in my head that you don't notice how hard this has been for me and I want to check that out, because I notice my Judge keep telling me, 'Chris should just know what you're going through.'

I'm sharing this because I want us to feel like a team. I value our partnership and want to work together to make things feel more balanced. Can you let me know earlier when you'll be late so I can plan ahead? And can we come up with a way to divide evening tasks so I'm not handling everything alone?

What did you notice about my request or what I shared?"

TRUTH EMPOWERED SPEAKING

Truth Empowered Listening.

NOTE: Chris doesn't ask Taylor a Clarifying Question—"What specifically feels hardest for Taylor on evenings without me?"—and a Curious Question—"How can I support Taylor in feeling their loneliness when I'm busy?" In your Truth Empowered Convos, ask CQs as the first part of your Report, before The Words.

Also: imagine you're Taylor. Wouldn't simply being asked those questions feel like Chris cares? Remember: ABC—Always Be Curious.

The Questions:

- WHAT SPECIFICALLY FEELS HARDEST FOR TAYLOR ON EVENINGS WITHOUT ME?
- HOW CAN I SUPPORT TAYLOR IN FEELING THEIR LONELINESS WHEN I'M BUSY?

The Words:

- TAYLOR FEELS OVERWHELMED, LONELY, HURT, RESENTFUL—<u>UNSUPPORTED</u>
- WANTS BETTER COMMUNICATION ABOUT MY WORK SCHEDULE
- ASKING FOR SHARED RESPONSIBILITIES AT HOME

The Inner:

- FEELINGS; GUILT AND SADNESS HEARING TAYLOR'S STRUGGLE
- SABOTEUR; "YOU'RE FAILING AS A PARTNER"
- REACTIONS; DEFENSIVE URGE TO JUSTIFY MY LATE NIGHTS; CALMING MYSELF TO FOCUS ON TAYLOR
- THOUGHTS; "THEY'RE NOT WRONG; I'VE BEEN ABSENT THIS WEEK"

The Outer:

- CALM VOICE, BUT THERE'S SOME TENSION.
- STEADY EYE CONTACT, SITTING UPRIGHT.
- A BIT OF SHAKINESS IN THEIR TONE—NERVOUS MAYBE? HURT?

The Undercurrents:

- I SENSE GENUINE CARE AND A DESIRE TO WORK TOGETHER.
- THEIR TONE CARRIES SHAKINESS AND TENSION BUT NO HOSTILITY.

HOST'S SAMPLE SHARE

"Taylor, I really appreciate you sharing this with me, especially since you said you were nervous to bring it up.

Here's what I heard: This week, I worked late every night, and you were left managing dinner, homework, and bedtime alone without a heads-up from me. That's left you feeling overwhelmed, lonely, hurt, and even kind of resentful. And you're asking me to communicate my schedule earlier, and for us to figure out a more balanced way to handle evening tasks. Did I get that right?

First off, I share your intention. So: while you spoke, I noticed a pang of guilt because I hate that my late nights have left you feeling what sounds to me like unsupported. I heard my Saboteur say 'You're failing as a partner.' I saw the impulse to jump in and defend myself, but I'm glad I held back because I see how much this matters to you.

I also took in that, even though your voice seemed to me a little shaky and tense—was that nervousness?—your tone was calm and caring. That showed me how much you value our partnership and want us to feel more like a team.

Here's what I commit to: I'll let you know as soon as I realize I'll be working late, and I'd love to sit down together this weekend to come up with a plan for sharing evening tasks. What do you notice about that idea, or anything else I said? Is there more you want to add?"

TRUTH EMPOWERED LISTENING

TRUTH EMPOWERED CONVOS: *Why they work*

Brain science says the structure of a Truth Empowered Convo creates a truly safe space to be seen and heard. Here's how.

When someone really listens with their full attention, it lights up your anterior cingulate cortex and **insula**—brain regions responsible for deeper self-awareness. That's why you might suddenly find yourself sharing insights you didn't even know you had. The act of being deeply listened to lets you discover clarity within yourself.

This kind of focus can feel intense and vulnerable. But the magic of neuroplasticity makes you start associating openness and honesty with feelings of safety, rather than judgment. Over time, this reshapes how you communicate: trust and connection feel like natural responses instead of risky leaps.

As a listener, when the Host stays tuned in—curious, present and open—it activates **mirror neurons**, which cultivate deep empathy and connection. It's as if you can feel each other's emotions on a real, almost physical level. These mirror neurons give rise to a profound **emotional attunement**, which feels like your two nervous systems are resonating in sync.

The intensity of this shared focus and vulnerability can forge a unique bond. It's sort of like the emotional closeness that's often associated with a trauma bond—except in this case, the bond forms through life-affirming honesty and mutual trust, not shared pain or adversity. Instead of reinforcing tension, your mutual openness releases it, giving you both an experience of freedom and safety.

A Truth Empowered Convo can be as healing as it is intimidating. But over time, the scary part fades, leaving a relationship that's fully rooted in safety, trust and mutual growth.

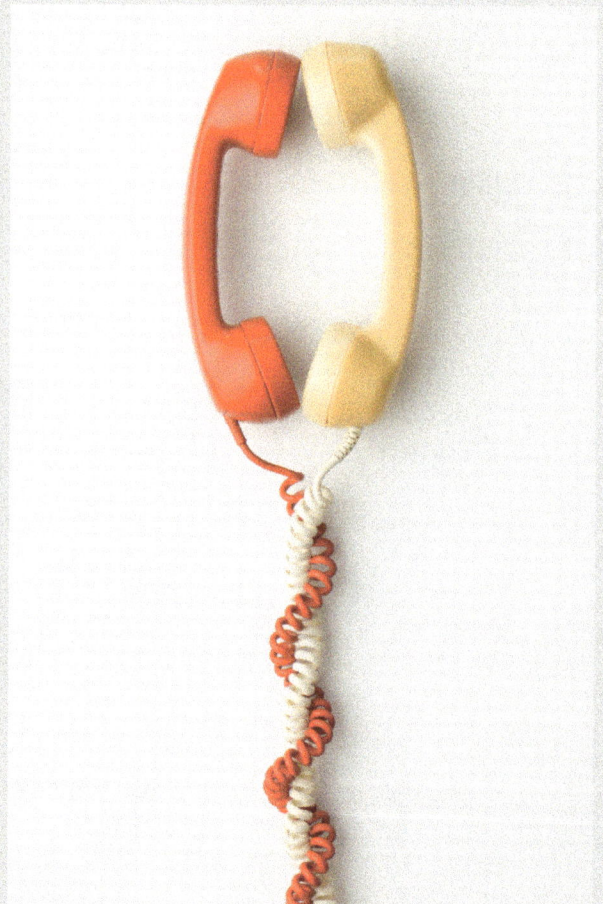

> **"THE QUIETER YOU BECOME, THE MORE YOU CAN HEAR."**
> **—RAM DASS**

TALK SHOW

Reflections

- *Reflections are most effective immediately after your convo*
- *Each player gets a chance to answer each question*
- *When you're done, advance to Level 05.*

	QUESTION	PLAYER 1	PLAYER 2
01	WHAT WAS THE CONVERSATION LIKE FOR YOU?	☐	☐
02	WHAT WAS CHALLENGING FOR YOU?	☐	☐
03	WHAT WAS EASY FOR YOU?	☐	☐
04	WHAT DID YOU LEARN ABOUT YOU?	☐	☐
05	WHAT DID YOU LEARN ABOUT ME?	☐	☐
06	WHAT DID YOU LEARN ABOUT SPEAKING?	☐	☐
07	WHAT DID YOU LEARN ABOUT LISTENING?	☐	☐
08	IN WHAT AREA OF SPEAKING DO YOU NEED THE MOST PRACTICE, AND WHY?	☐	☐
09	IN WHAT AREA OF LISTENING DO YOU NEED THE MOST PRACTICE, AND WHY?	☐	☐

LEVEL

05

THE INSTRUCTIONS: KEEPING YOU PSYCHOLOGICALLY SAFE | 15 PAGES + WORKSHEET

What you will learn

These guidelines keep your Truth Empowered Convos grounded, sensitive and real. With them in place, you and your partner can be fully open, because you've created an environment that's psychologically safe. Though real honesty still takes bravery, the Instructions make things a whole lot easier.

"THE ULTIMATE TEST OF A RELATIONSHIP IS TO *hold hands* WHILE YOU *disagree.*"

—INSPIRED BY ALEXANDRA PENNEY

Congratulations—you've learned to be both the Host and Guest in *Talk Show*. That was your first **Truth Empowered Convo**. You now know how to have one.

The Instructions establish a psycholigically safe relationship. Just like the rules that come with a board game, they make sure you both feel supported, understood, and fully engaged while you play the fascinatingly intricate game of deep intimacy.

Each Instruction is fundamental to this approach—and each one will ask you to commit anew to having a Truth Empowered Relationship.

So here's the plan: let's have a *Talk Show* for each Instruction.

As Host and Guest, explore each Instruction. Talk through what it means to you, any reactions or feelings or questions it brings up, and make sure you both understand it and **agree to it**.

These are ten more opportunities to make sure you're both on the same page—and ten more opportunities to understand each other in new ways.

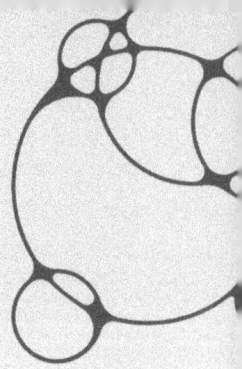

You're ready to talk

THE INSTRUCTIONS:
Your emotional safety net

The Instructions act as an emotional safety net. They calm the amygdala, which is sensitive to judgment or rejection, and engage the prefrontal cortex—the hub of logic, empathy, and adaptability. Conversations become supportive instead of defensive.

Remember mirror neurons? They help us tune into and understand each other's emotions. The curiosity-driven, empathetic responses the Instructions generate activates these mirror neurons, creating a natural sense of connection on a neurological level.

When you consistently follow the Instructions, it's like sending a safety signal to the limbic system, telling it "This is a safe zone, not a war zone." The limbic system then plays its part in regulating your emotions: stress responses are replaced by emotional stability. Over time, when your new neuronal pathways strengthen, living in alignment with these Instructions takes less effort and becomes more automatic.

Following the Instructions also triggers the release of oxytocin, that bonding hormone. It promotes closeness and lowers stress. The calming effect can be a great relief when you're having challenging conversations.

THE INSTRUCTIONS CAN RESHAPE THE WAY YOU INTERACT.

You'll also build your EQ, boosting your ability to relate. Plus, research shows that empathetic and self-aware conversations strengthen resilience, making conflicts easier to navigate.

These Instructions weave a powerful web of mutual support, protecting you both as you grow together. Think of them as a relationship referee who's on both your sides—rooting for you both to become your best selves, and build an unbreakable connection.

The Instructions:

01 OWN YOUR EMOTIONS

You are responsible for your inner world. No one can 'make' you feel anything; your emotions belong to you. Whether you feel angry, sad, frustrated—acknowledge those emotions and explore their source: they're there for a reason. Find out why. Own your feelings, and let your partner own theirs.

02 DON'T FIX—LISTEN

When your partner is sharing a feeling or experience, resist the urge to fix, solve, or give advice. Instead, offer presence. True support is not 'fixing' your partner's emotions—it's holding space for them to express and process their truth. Be a witness, not a mechanic.

03 SEEK UNDERSTANDING, NOT AGREEMENT

Imagine paddling down a river in a canoe. Agreement might feel like using your oars in perfect sync, but understanding is about working together to adapt to the river's twists and turns: one person steers, the other adds power. It's not about doing the same thing; it's about moving forward as a team—even when your perspectives are different.

04 SET INTENTIONS

Before a Truth Empowered Convo, set a clear intention: to listen with your whole being maybe, or to express your truth without hiding, or to create mutual understanding. Your intention becomes a compass, guiding your words and actions. It keeps you focused on what really matters to you.

05 CURIOSITY OVER ASSUMPTIONS OR JUDGMENT

Assumptions are like trying to guess the image on a puzzle with only a few pieces in place—they create misunderstandings. Genuine curiosity helps fill in the missing pieces, so you get an accurate picture. Notice when you're assuming instead of being curious. Also, practice radical non-judgment when you listen: no feeling, thought or perspective is wrong. If you catch yourself judging, note it, accept it, and shift back to curiosity.

YOUR EMOTIONAL SAFETY NET

PRACTICE ELEVATION AWARENESS 06

Remember, if emotions heighten during a convo, it's essential to notice and address it. If either of you seem elevated, ask, "Are you [Am I] getting elevated?" If yes, take a breath, say "I feel [angry, hurt]," and explore why. Expressing your emotions re-grounds the convo, bringing the elevator back down.

MUTUAL CARE AND RESPECT 07

At the heart of Truth Empowered Relationships is mutual care. Treat your partner's emotions, needs and boundaries with the same level of respect and care you want for yourself. When both partners actively demonstrate care and respect, a dynamic of trust is created that strengthens the relationship.

EMBRACE THE POWER OF APOLOGY 08

Mistakes are inevitable. What counts is how you address them. A Truth Empowered Apology takes three steps: owning your actions without defensiveness, explaining your intent without excuses, and committing to a plan for growth. This shows your partner their trust is more important to you than your ego.

EMBRACE THE POWER OF FORGIVENESS 09

They don't give out prizes for being tolerant in a relationship. Recognize mistreatment. But your partner's Truth Empowered Apology—taking responsibility, finding and sharing the why, and learning from it—shows they're conscious, evolving and committed to growth. I say that's someone worth forgiving.

ALWAYS SPEAK YOUR TRUTH CONSCIOUSLY 10

When you speak your truth, always use the structure of Truth Empowered Speaking. This isn't about restricting your voice; it's about creating clarity, and minimizing misunderstandings and defensiveness. By staying within this framework, your words are more likely to be truly heard and respected. That leads to *more* willingness to have *more* open, honest convos.

abo ut

inte ntio ns

Setting intentions can profoundly affect your relationships—and your overall well-being.

Intentions don't eliminate misunderstandings —they're a natural part of conversations. But intentions activate the RAS, which sharpens focus, reduces distractions, and keeps you aligned with what matters to you. You'll navigate those moments with more grace.

Let's say you set an intention before a convo to build mutual understanding, You'll likely listen more deeply and choose words with more care, creating emotional safety.

Intentions also boost comprehension, reduce defensiveness, and foster problem-solving. And they coordinate your actions and words with your wants, inviting mindful manifesting into your life. So set them regularly, and you'll start creating the life you desire.

Try it: before your next convo, set an intention for the outcome you want. Say your intention out loud too: sharing it at the end of The Under reassures the listener.

Intentions can shape connections and transform conversations.

Before you engage, pause and reflect: *What's my intention here?*

On Selfish MOTIVATIONS

Around age 36, Mother Teresa, now canonized as Saint Teresa of Calcutta, believed she heard the voice of God, urging her to serve the poor, the sick and diseased, the abandoned and unloved.

But after she dedicated herself to this mission, what she experienced as her connection to the divine suddenly vanished. Unbeknownst to the world watching her tireless efforts, Mother Teresa was grappling with spiritual darkness and a profound sense of loss. Her diary, revealed after her death, documents her years of longing for God's presence: she repeatedly asks God why her connection to Him disappeared, and if He can see how hard she's working to win it back.

Saint Teresa's moving and inspiring work wasn't only for others; it was also a plea to regain her own lost sense of divine intimacy. Her inner pain and outer actions are the ultimate illustration of my point: selfish motives are intertwined with all selfless deeds.

COME-FROMS

I often reference this story because many people defend the concept of altruism: acting out of selflessness or nobility. In a Truth Empowered Relationship, knowing your selfish motivations and being upfront about them matters deeply. When you're transparent, your partner can better understand your **come-from**: *why* you're saying or doing something. "You look like you could use a hug," for instance, has a different come-from than "Hugging you when you're down fills me up."

Recognizing and expressing your motivations can ease cognitive dissonance—the tension when actions clash with beliefs. Being transparent calms your amygdala, and engages the prefrontal cortex, helping you think clearly, so you're more conscious in conversations—which encourages empathy from your partner. Everybody wins.

A SIGNAL OF TRUST

The Stoics practiced self-examination daily: they believed that uncovering the intentions driving their actions led to wisdom. Indigenous traditions honor when people are transparent with their intentions, considering it essential to respect and trust. When we say "This is why I'm doing what I'm doing"—even when the reason's messy or selfish—we signal we're self-aware. Defenses lower. Exchanges get infused with clarity.

LYING VS. WITHHOLDING

WHAT'S THE DIFFERENCE AND WHY DOES IT MATTER?

Truth Empowered Relationships considers lying and withholding as the same, because both have the same impact on your nervous system and your relationship.

Our brains crave consistency. When one person withholds information—even info that seems harmless—the other's intuition will often pick up on that disconnect. Their brain knows something isn't adding up. That's cognitive dissonance, and it can spike anxiety and stress. Outright lie or quiet omission, the acute stress response kicks in because your nervous system senses danger in the inconsistency.

Psychologically, both lying and withholding will break down trust. When you're not fully open, your partner senses it, and that creates energetic distance and weakens connection. It's like throwing a wrench into the gears of trust. A Truth Empowered Relationship needs the emotional safety of transparency to thrive.

Traditions like Buddhism believe withholding truth is just another form of dishonesty. It blocks the natural flow between people, making it more difficult to feel close.

So the next time you're considering holding something back, remember: lie or withhold, the effect's the same—nervous systems are stressed and trust takes a hit. But leaning into the full truth is like fixing a loose wire: the current flows again, and the natural circuit of your bond is restored. Second-guessing and uneasiness are replaced with the unique calm that only trust can bring.

FEELING VS. FACT

WHICH ONE GETS PRIORITY AND WHY?

In Truth Empowered Relationships, understanding someone's feelings before addressing the facts is key to real communication. Here's why: when someone's upset, their body experiences the acute stress response—that heightened state where their logical brain essentially shuts down. In that state, the prefrontal cortex, responsible for logic and reasoning, is offline—the emotional brain, chiefly the amygdala, has taken over. So simply put, when someone's emotionally charged, **their brain isn't ready to process facts until their feelings are acknowledged.**

Emotions are like a blaring alarm in the brain. Without addressing the feelings behind the alarm, reasoning gets drowned out. But empathizing—"I get why this is frustrating for you" or "I can see why you're upset"—effectively turns off the alarm. This signals the nervous system to calm, activating the parasympathetic system, which induces relaxation and recovery. Research shows validating emotions not only lowers cortisol levels, but also rewires the brain to process future emotions in healthier ways.

Studies of EQ agree: feelings should be addressed before facts. Empathy creates an environment where brain and body feel safe enough to engage in meaningful conversation. In short, empathizing says "I'm with you." Once someone feels that emotional security, they're far more likely to process facts, because the emotional barriers are down.

Feelings and facts deserve equal weight. Feelings reveal our inner truth, while facts illuminate the path forward. But ignoring or skipping over feelings to focus on facts creates distance. **Meet the emotional reality first**. That opens the door for the brain to process facts. When feelings are tended to first, understanding and clarity naturally follow.

it's time to play

TALK SHOW: INSTRUCTIONS

<u>Truth Empowered Convos</u> **about each of The Instructions**

TALK SHOW: INSTRUCTIONS

FOR 2 PLAYERS

SUGGESTED LENGTH 1-2 HOURS

OBJECT OF THE GAME

Discuss and commit to the ten Instructions that will transform your interactions, creating safe, conscious, respectful and deeply constructive conversations.

HOW TO PLAY

Rock Paper Scissors to be Player 1, who starts as Guest. Alternate who goes first for each of the ten Instructions.

Dive into each of The Instructions using the *Talk Show* format, one Truth Empowered Convo at a time. Allow 10 minutes minimum for each Convo. For each Instruction, ask:

- What feelings or thoughts surfaced about this Instruction?
- What saboteurs did you notice?
- What impulses did you notice?
- Do you find anything about this Instruction challenging?
- Is there anything about it that needs clarifying?
- Are you both ready to commit to it?

Agree that, for now, these conversations honor The Instructions. Speak with awareness, listen actively, and own your emotions. By doing this, you'll already be putting into practice the very principles that, if you both agree to adhere to them, will create a safe, connected space for both of you.

Afterwards, reflect using the prompts on the following page.

Reflections

- **Reflections are most effective immediately after your convo**
- **Each player gets a chance to answer each question**
- **When you're done, read the next three pages, then advance to Level 06.**

---

01   WHAT WAS THE CONVERSATION LIKE FOR YOU?   YOU ☐   ME ☐

---

02   WHAT WAS CHALLENGING FOR YOU?   YOU ☐   ME ☐

---

03   WHAT WAS EASY FOR YOU?   YOU ☐   ME ☐

---

04   WHAT DID YOU LEARN ABOUT YOU?   YOU ☐   ME ☐

---

05   WHAT DID YOU LEARN ABOUT ME?   YOU ☐   ME ☐

---

06   WHAT DO YOU WANT TO EXPRESS ABOUT LYING VS. WITHHOLDING?   YOU ☐   ME ☐

---

07   WHAT DO YOU WANT TO EXPRESS ABOUT FEELINGS VS. FACTS?   YOU ☐   ME ☐

---

08   WHAT QUESTIONS REMAIN FOR YOU ABOUT THE INSTRUCTIONS?   YOU ☐   ME ☐

---

09   IMAGINE HAVING OUR RELATIONSHIP ABIDE BY THESE RULES. WHAT WILL IT FEEL LIKE?   YOU ☐   ME ☐

WE'RE STILL GETTING TRIGGERED IN OUR CONVERSATIONS

Getting triggered is normal. It simply means our nervous system is sensing potential danger based on past events. We need to notice and open to these triggers—and understand their origins—to deactivate them.

If a trigger is causing one of you to get elevated, that person should voice what they're feeling. If they don't, the other partner gently asks, "You seem elevated—are you?" If the answer's 'yes,' ask "What's the feeling?" Then find out what's behind it.

WE'RE CHALLENGED BY APOLOGIES OR FORGIVENESS

If your partner's apology seems empty to you, say that, responsibly: "I didn't feel your apology. What was your inner world like when you apologized?"

If you feel pressured to forgive quickly but you're not there yet, say that: "I heard your apology, but I'm not ready to forgive yet." Then let time pass. Forgiveness is a process and doesn't always happen immediately. Sharing your resentments after the apology can also help you truly forgive.

MY PARTNER ISN'T FOLLOWING THE INSTRUCTIONS

The Instructions create psychological safety—**they're not optional.** Think of them as a built-in referee who's on both of your sides.

Have a *Talk Show* convo about that partner's resistance to that Instruction. If one of you disputes that they're not following an Instruction, invite an open discussion about perspectives: "Let's explore how this looks from both our points of view."

EVEN AFTER THAT CONVO, NOTHING SHIFTED

If nothing shifts, I suggest your next discussion be about whether or not this method is a fit for your relationship. As we've talked about, Truth Empowered Relationships requires both partners to want conscious intimacy.

A Truth Empowered Relationship cannot be one-sided. I've seen many couples where only one partner wants conscious intimacy. I've never seen that scenario work out. Conscious intimacy requires mutual commitment.

A **poke** is a subtle jab aimed at tender spots: unresolved wounds, hidden resentments, or past pain points. Pokes are forms of micro-aggression designed to sting—though they're often made unconsciously. They breach the trust that's essential to a Truth Empowered Relationship. Pokes emerge when we don't address our underlying frustrations directly; instead, we use veiled references to past conflicts, or to our partner's vulnerabilities. The result: our emotional tension gets offloaded—at the cost of connection.

The POKE

THE UNCONSCIOUS ATTACK

Pokes are driven by emotional triggers rooted in the limbic system, the brain's emotional headquarters.

The amygdala, like an emotional smoke detector, reacts instantly with fear, anger or anxiety to perceived threats. This split-second response is great when there's a tiger in the bushes—but not so helpful with modern stressors like arguments or perceived slights, which can also trigger the amygdala. So if the brain perceives a pattern that resembles past pain, the heightened nervous system may launch a poke as a rapid-fire response.

Then there's the DMN, which can stew over unresolved conflicts when activated. That sparks those pokes that are endless replays of past dramas: "Remember when you forgot my birthday?" or "Must be nice to have time for *your* hobbies." It's like the brain gets stuck on a playlist of meanness.

Level 06 lays out the four Pillars of Truth Empowered Relationships, including **Non-Meanness**, the 'do no harm' principle. Pokes violate this principle because they harm—intentionally or unintentionally.

Healing starts by taking responsibility for the harm: own up to and apologize for the poke, then deactivate its charge by exploring and explaining the emotions behind it: jealousy, insecurity, loneliness.

Bring these truths to light and you'll disarm pokes at the source. Pokes aren't just jabs—they're breadcrumbs leading back to a need, a hurt, a fear. Exploring pokes as a couple can prevent future ones, and not just repair your bond but fortify it—in the same way that a bone heals stronger after a fracture.

What pokes have you made in your relationship? Where do they come from?

"I need a lazy day"

ON THE DAYS YOU JUST DON'T WANT TO FOLLOW A STRUCTURE

Truth Empowered Convos are deep and structured. Some days, you just might not have one in you. On those days, say out loud: "I need a lazy day." You're respecting your own energy, while also alerting your partner not to rely on the structure that day.

You can spend a Lazy Day together in quiet companionship—just being in each other's presence—or apart, each doing what restores your peace. Be honest with yourselves and each other about whether you want company or to go solo during this unstructured time.

You still abide by the Instructions and Pillars. But you keep conversations light, so you can honor your need for rest, while still maintaining your mutual respect and your connection.

If you've chosen to stick together on a Lazy Day, and things start to get tense, just say "Lazy Day!" as a gentle reminder of the vibe you called for: a break from conversations that go deep. If things stay tense, try a Lazy Day Timeout: some time apart to reset.

Each of you can call one Lazy Day per week. That limit makes sure you're still focused on building the muscle memory of conscious communication—so that intimacy becomes so effortless, you don't *need* Lazy Days.

LEVEL

06

THE PILLARS: CORNERSTONES OF ETHICAL LOVE

14 PAGES

LET'S GO!

What you will learn

The Pillars, inspired by medical ethics, bring a foundation of healing into your relationship. When you both embody them, you become each other's therapist, coach, best friend, and passion partner—and your own as well. A relationship rooted in the Pillars nurtures both individual and shared well-being

"*Love* IS A VESSEL THAT CONTAINS BOTH *security* AND *adventure*"

—ESTHER PEREL

THE PILLARS

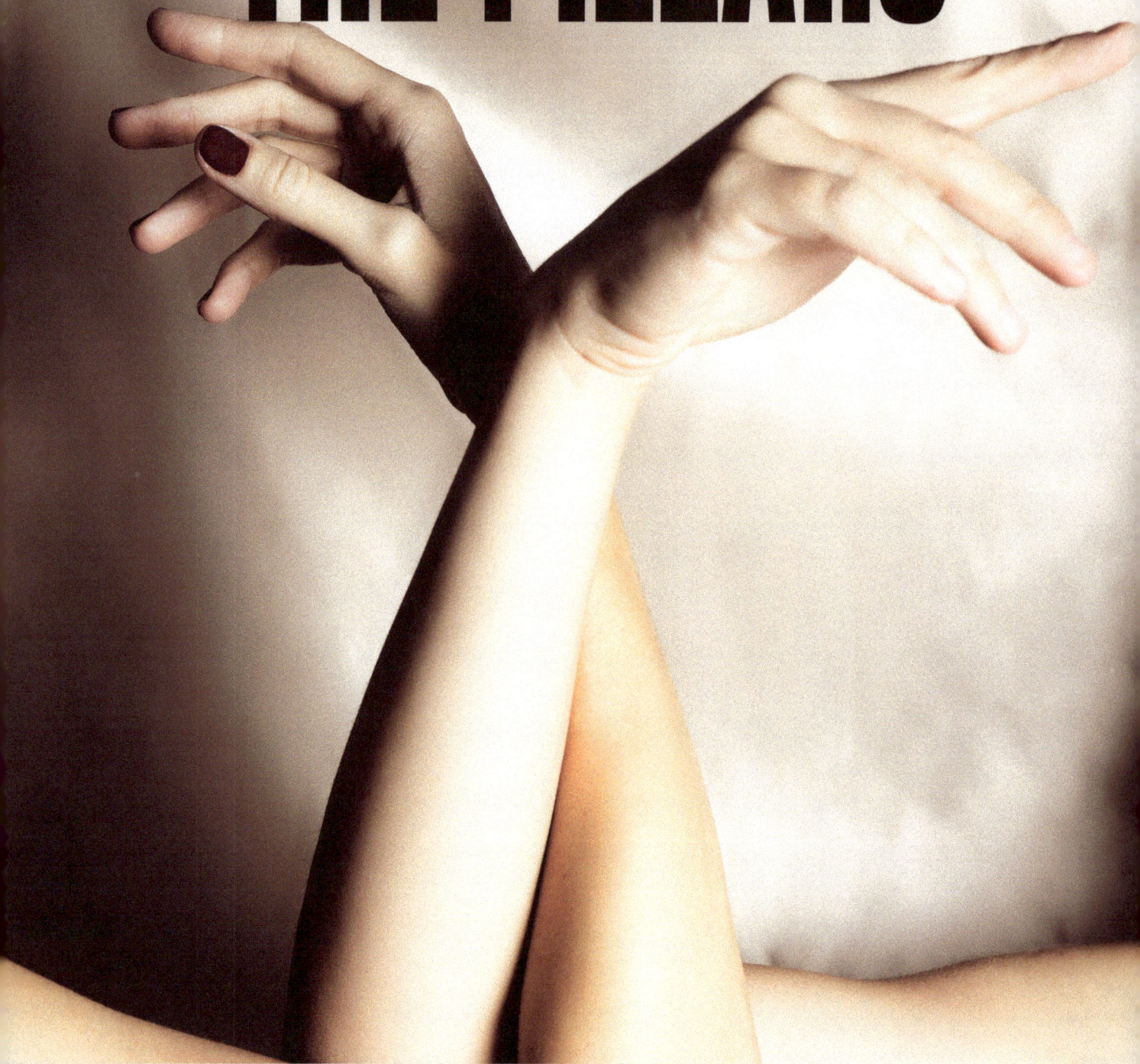

The four Pillars of Truth Empowered Relationships—Freeness, Wholesomeness, Non-Meanness, and Fairness—are borrowed from medical ethics but made for love.

The Pillars work hand-in-hand with the Instructions, by offering a deeper moral foundation for your relationship. While the Instructions give practical guidance to shape your behavior and interactions, the Pillars are a philosophical framework for creating a connection that's a healing sanctuary, anchored in mutual respect and a commitment to your growth as humans.

When you embrace these Pillars, you'll cheer each other on like best friends, offer honest feedback like supportive coaches, bring clarity like caring therapists, and keep the spark alive as passion partners. Your relationship will nurture you both in every way, from the heart to the soul and everywhere in between. You'll feel safe to be your truest selves—while you evolve into your most fully realized selves

How the Pillars give your relationship
AN ETHICAL STRUCTURE

I created the Pillars to parallel the ancient principles of medical ethics. A professional caregiver's goal isn't just to fix problems—it's to nurture well-being, minimize harm, and honor each person's choices. The Pillars are rooted in that same spirit of care. That's why they can they resuscitate your relationship, breathe life into it, keep its heartbeat strong.

- **Freeness** parallels *autonomy* in medical ethics: you celebrate who your partner is, instead of trying to mold them into who you think they should be.
- **Wholesomeness** aligns with *beneficence*: actively doing good to enrich each other's lives.
- **Non-Meanness** mirrors *non-maleficence*: removing cruelty from your words, your actions and your energy in interactions.
- **Fairness** echoes *justice*: making sure your partnership is equal, with mutual respect and shared responsibility.

These ideas show up across cultures and philosophies. Buddhism's "right speech?" That's Non-Meanness. Indigenous traditions of reciprocal care? That's Wholesomeness.

So the Pillars aren't just some modern relationship hack. They tap into the universal human desire to love and be loved in ways that honor our shared humanity.

And here's what makes them truly healing: they insist that you see your partner as a **whole person**—not just someone who exists to meet your needs.

So how do the Pillars and Instructions sync?

Think of it like this: The Instructions tell you **how**: they're a step-by-step guide to building an ethical relationship. The Pillars tell you **why**: they anchor you in the values that inspire those steps—and every step you take together.

If the Instructions are your GPS, giving you turn-by-turn directions for daily life together, the Pillars are your compass, always pointing you toward the kind of relationship you want to create.

Together, they elevate relationships, taking them from transactional to transformational.

It's been said that when we fall in love with someone, we put a box around them: our expectations of them, conscious or unconscious, when it comes to love. As long as they stay in our box, we love them. When they move outside of our box, we punish them—until they get back into our box, and then we love them again. Does that box sound like love to you? It doesn't to me.

Freeness says: love has no box.

Freeness is the magic of loving someone for exactly who they are, without trying to mold, steer or control them. It's the quiet joy of watching your partner chase their dreams, make their choices, and express themselves fully—seeing their autonomy not as a threat, but as a vital part of your connection.

Here's just one way freeness is present in our marriage: Heather moved 16 times growing up. Every school year, all her childhood, she was 'the new kid.' I've heard her stories of what it was like, and I wouldn't wish that on any kid.

A byproduct of that life: Heather never got to make friends. So having friends has a different meaning to her now than it would for most people her age. I always encourage her to go out with her friends, even when she feels guilty about it—and even if, on some days, I'd rather have her home with me. Freeness means I want her to do what *she* wants, not what *I* want.

Now, even if she hadn't had moved so much, and had a stadium full of friends, I'd give her that same encouragement. I don't put a box around Heather. All I expect is that she follows the Structure, Instructions and Pillars. The resulting flow of love between us is so strong, it nurtures me every second of every day, whether I'm focused on it or not.

What does Freeness require? That I take responsibility for my own emotions. If I miss Heather when she's out, that's *my* loneliness to sit with. If I feel jealous, that's *my* insecurity to look at. And yes, even when I'm left figuring out my own dinner (by far the toughest part for me), my hunger is mine to solve too.

What happens when we don't embrace Freeness? When we try to restrict our partner, make them responsible for our emotions instead of trusting ourselves to sit with them? That's when you'll hear resentful comments like "You never let me [FILL IN THE BLANK]."

Putting your partner in the box paradigm means making them be as *you* want them to be, or as *you* believe they should be. It's like putting them in a prison where you're the warden.

If you're unhappy with your partner as they are, I say **leave**. And be aware: your partner may not stop you—prisoners often don't like wardens.

Love isn't about guards and gates. Freeness transforms your relationship from a prison to a partnership. It creates a love that's not about holding on—it's about giving each other room to grow. Research says relationships built on mutual autonomy are happier and healthier. And it's no wonder: when you feel free to be yourself, you bring your best, most vibrant self to the table.

If you've been living inside someone else's box of love—or if you've put a box around someone—Freeness says: knock it down. Trust your partner to follow their own guidance. Individual freeness results in shared strength.

What boxes have you lived in—or put around your partner? What would happen if you knocked them down?

Imagine you're camping. With flint and a few sticks, you start a fire. It's small and modest.

Now imagine your partner comes back with logs and adds them to the fire. It'll burn longer and more brightly. And what happens if your partner stops adding logs? The fire dims. The embers cool. The glow fades.

Wholesomeness says: love adds.

Wholesomeness is love as a verb: an ongoing, conscious practice of adding goodness to each other's lives. Each act of kindness, care, and contribution—a heartfelt compliment when they're doubting themselves, or folding the laundry when you can tell they're exhausted—is another log that keeps the fire burning bright and warm. When you actively seek to enrich your partner's life, you're not just nurturing them— you're nurturing your connection.

Heather and I have a ritual where we both express Wholesomeness at the same time. Almost every night of our lives, laying in bed together, she and I have given each other healing massages or loving touches. As I give to her, I also receive from her; as I receive, I'm more fueled to give. It's a feedback loop of love that makes us both feel more whole. I said "almost" every night: sometimes Heather's shoulder hurts. That's when I give her extra rubs— because she needs extra logs on her fire.

Wholesomeness is that simple: the small gestures that say, "I see you, I care about you, and I'm invested in your happiness." It's a dependable flow of positive contributions that make your partner's well-being part of your daily life—not to fix their day, but to add to their sense of safety and care.

Wholesomeness: LOVE BY ADDITION

Wholesomeness means your presence is a net positive in your partner's world. Just like adding a steady supply of logs keeps a fire burning, adding your small, consistent contributions keeps your relationship's fire burning. Studies say small acts of kindness in a relationship build trust, satisfaction and resilience.

But Wholesomeness isn't just the actions themselves—it's the mindset behind them. It's asking yourself, "How can I contribute to my partner's well-being today?" without expecting anything in return—except that warm feeling giving to someone else provides.

It might be a kind word, a shared laugh, a thoughtful gesture. It might be stepping back to let them solve a problem on their own, or stepping in to offer support they didn't even know they needed. In a world that often measures love by what we get, Wholesomeness focuses on what we give.

Wholesomeness means valuing your partner's well-being as equal to your own—not more, not less. Yes, be actively caring and generous with your time, attention, and support—but not when you don't have it to give. When your acts of Wholesomeness come from obligation or duty, they'll drain your bond. Acts that come from generosity, by contrast, nurture your connection.

Embracing Wholesomeness creates a love that isn't just sustaining—it's enriching. That kind of love always grows and strengthens—because both partners are committed to adding their unique fuel to their partner's fire.

What Wholesomeness logs are you adding to your relationship fire? What could you add today to make your love burn even brighter?

Picture yourself in front of a wooden fence, with a hammer and a box of nails. You pound the nails into the fence with the blunt end of the hammer. Then you pull them out with the forked end.

Being mean to your partner—like the Pokes we talked about in Level 05—is like pounding nails into that fence. Apologizing is like pulling them out.

But notice something about that fence: when you pull the nails out, it's full of holes. That's what meanness does to a relationship over time—fills it with holes.

Non-Meanness says: do no harm.

Non-Meanness means you do nothing to damage your partner's well-being. It's more than just avoiding cruelty or aggression; it's intentionally creating a sanctuary of respect, where you both feel safe to be vulnerable—especially when emotions run high. Because even in moments of anger, your partner's humanity deserves your honor. When we live by Non-Meanness, we become guardians of our partner's hearts.

With Heather, this means holding back reflexive comments when I'm triggered. For example, if she sighs when I'm sharing something, my thoughts might be, "Don't I matter to you?" or "Am I boring you?" But Non-Meanness asks me to pause and reflect: what's the truth under those thoughts? That I'm hurt because I want her empathy about my experiences. So I say, "When you sighed, I made up that what I said didn't matter to you, and I really need your empathy." It builds closeness instead of creating distance—and I find out, as I often have, that her sighs almost *never* have anything to do with me.

Here's a Non-Meanness hack: when we start feeling triggered in a conversation,

one of us says "pause," so we don't say things we don't mean, or act in ways we'd regret. We stop, take a breath, and return to the talk with calm and care.

If you do act in a way that causes harm, Non-Meanness asks you to **own your impact.** Mere apologies still leave holes in the fence. Owning your impact means also explaining why you caused harm, and what your new intention is if that trigger comes up again. That willingness to repair helps soothe your partner's amygdala, restoring their emotional equilibrium and trust.

Embracing Non-Meanness can put an end to manipulation, dismissiveness, criticism and pokes—all of which chip away at trust. Non-Meanness keeps that fence we're guarding from becoming full of nails—or, best case scenario, full of holes. Relationships that don't embrace this Pillar often become battlegrounds, where winning an argument matters more than preserving connection.

Non-Meanness asks you to be mindful: catch those moments where a snide remark or sarcastic jab feels tempting, and choose connection over conflict. Couples who practice Non-Meanness during conflict report more satisfying and longer-lasting relationships.

Adopting Non-Meanness doesn't mean bottling up your feelings. It means expressing them responsibly. Instead of attacking, you voice your frustrations. Instead of lashing out, you share your discomfort. Even when you're triggered, you keep your partner's heart safe. This preserves the strength of a bond built on respect—and demonstrates that you hold your love as sacred.

What might you have done or said to cause your partner harm? How can you honor their humanity, even in tension?

Non-Meanness: LOVE WITH HONOR

Pretend you're both on a seesaw. To create that playful rhythm of balance, you both need to contribute your weight and energy. If one of you decides to stay on the ground, the other's suspended and trapped...unless they jump off.

Fairness says: love must stay balanced.

Fairness is the art of making sure both partners feel equally valued, heard and supported. You each have different needs, dreams and capacities—and that's okay. It's not about splitting everything 50/50—it's about figuring out the way each of you can give that makes the most of your gifts, while also factoring in your energy and time.

Fairness asks you to recognize and respect the unique ways each of you contributes—and to be willing to adapt when life changes the weight on one side of the seesaw. With Fairness, both of your needs matter, and neither of you feels overburdened or overlooked.

Here's an example of how Fairness plays out in our relationship: when it comes to housework, I'm not exactly what you'd call a natural. In addition, I have vision issues. Heather, on the other hand, has an organic knack for organization and cleanliness—and she sees everything.

Dishes and bills were my responsibility. But Heather shared, with honesty and care, that she was bothered by spots I missed, and that she enjoys paying bills. So she took over both tasks.

Immediately it seemed unfair to simply let her add those tasks to her long list of magical contributions. So I said, "Then I'm taking over laundry." She said, "I'm not asking you to." I said, "I know. I'm doing it anyway." (I have to go put in a load as I type this.) I also took over her share of a task I enjoy: mowing the lawn.

LOVE SEES BOTH SIDES
Fairness:

It wasn't about balancing the hours spent working. It was about balancing the effort, so she knows her well-being matters as much to me as mine.

When the weight on the seesaw changes —like when she was recovering from surgery—I carry more of the load. On the flip side, when I was writing this book, Heather took over some of my tasks. We're in this together, equal players on the same team. That also extends to emotional balance: when one of us needs extra support, the other one understands—and offers it willingly.

What does Fairness require? Self-awareness and communication: you both honestly assess whether you're carrying too much or too little of the load, and when things feel unbalanced, you speak up: "I need more help right now" or "I'm feeling overwhelmed." It's a mindset that says, "Let's do our parts." Studies show fairness is a predictor of relationship satisfaction.

Without Fairness, one of you may feel overburdened or undervalued, while the other feels unengaged or disconnected. Your relationship can become a tug-of-war over keeping score: "I do so much around here." Resentments like those signal your connection needs Fairness.

Fairness means bringing intention and care to your shared responsibilities. It's the antidote to those unspoken, unacknowledged inequalities that lead to resentment. Fairness invites you to lean into the give-and-receive of love: just like a seesaw, love needs motion and effort on both sides to stay fun and balanced. With Fairness, love is not a solo act—it's a partnership worth riding.

What dynamics in your relationship need rebalancing? How can you bring more fairness into your connection?

EMBRACING YOUR UNKNOWN

When "I don't know" is your truth, get used to saying it

My senior year at university, I had a 'role-playing' interview with AT&T: I pretended to already be an employee, going to meet with clients at a fictitious company. The 'clients,' however, were actually my interviewers.

To prepare, I read and re-read a four-page case study about the pretend company. Then the meeting began. It seemed to be going smoothly—until one 'client' asked a question that hadn't been covered in the case study. I wasn't sure what to do, but since I didn't know the answer, that's what I said: "I don't know. I'll find out when I get back to the 'office."

Then the other 'client' asked me a question that *also* hadn't been covered in the case study. Now I started to wonder: had I missed a page of that case study? Again, I said "I don't know that either. I'll call you when I get back to the office." It happened a *third* time, and once again I said I didn't know. I left the interview truly unsure how I did. But I got an offer.

At training, I ran into one of my interviewers. "I don't know if you remember me—" I started.

"Remember you?" She laughed. "I gave you the highest score anyone's ever gotten at AT&T."

At that time, AT&T employed over a million people. I was astonished. "Why?" I asked.

"Because no one's ever had the guts," she replied, "to say 'I don't know' all three times."

Admitting you don't know something can feel like weakness, especially if you've been mocked or ridiculed for not knowing. But the alternative is choosing confidence over competence—and that's led to the downfall of relationships, corporations, even nations.

The reality is, "I don't know" is *often* the **only true answer.** And since we committed to truth, if "I don't know" is the truth, then that's what we say: "I don't know how to answer that the way you phrased it." "I don't know if I want to do that—let me think about it."

"I don't know" tells your listener it's okay not to have all the answers—and that they don't have to hide *their* doubts. When you both admit when you don't know, a meaningful next step emerges, that's based on your actual truths.

So in your Pillar Talks—and in all your convos—when you don't know, say "I don't know." The irony is, you'll end up knowing much more.

PILLAR TALK

Pillar Talk is your chance to deepen connection through five guided Truth Empowered Convos, centered on the four Pillars of a Truth Empowered Relationship. Using the *Talk Show* format, and with prompt questions guiding you through each convo, you'll both share your inner realities and your perspectives about the Pillars.

The final conversation focuses on integrating the Pillars into your relationship for the long term—making sure both of you feel valued, seen, and inspired to adopt these principles as the guiding lights of your connection.

I suggest having no more than one conversation per night, to give each topic the space it deserves. If you prefer to take more time, that's perfectly fine—just be sure to schedule all five convos, so they remain a priority.

it's time to play

PILLAR TALK

Where you have Truth Empowered Convos about The Pillars

INTERMEDIATE

PILLAR TALK

FOR 2 PLAYERS

SUGGESTED LENGTH 1-2 HOURS

OBJECT OF THE GAME

Discuss and agree on the four Pillars that will form the heart of your relationship: how you view them, how you approach them, how you hold them in your heart.

HOW TO PLAY

Rock Paper Scissors to be Player 1, who starts the first convo as the Guest. Alternate for each convo.

Using the *Talk Show* format, have five Truth Empowered Convos about the Pillars. Allow 10 minutes for each convo.

Begin each *Pillar Talk* with these questions, to spark reflection:

- What feelings or thoughts arose as you read this Pillar?
- What saboteurs did you notice?
- What impulses?

The following page has **additional prompts for each Pillar.**

For the fifth convo, skip the questions above; use the prompts provided on the following page.

After your fifth *Pillar Talk*, **advance to Level 07.**

PILLAR TALK: *Additional prompts*

01 Freeness

- What does freeness in our relationship mean to you?
- Remember a time when your freeness wasn't respected. What was that like for you?
- What can we do to make sure neither of us feels held back or controlled?
- When do we make decisions alone vs. as a couple?

02 Wholesomeness

- What actions of mine support your well-being?
- Do you need support in other ways—emotional, mental, or physical?
- Are there needs I might be missing? What are they?
- What can we do regularly to boost wholesomeness?

03 Non-Meanness

- What does "do no harm" look like for us?
- Have there been times you've felt hurt by me, even unintentionally? Tell me about them.
- What words or actions from me feel hurtful to you?
- What would help you feel completely safe with me?

04 Fairness

- Do you believe we both contribute equally to this relationship? If not, what feels off-balance?
- What does fairness look like in our daily life?
- What can we do or be to keep our needs and desires equally important?

05 Adopting the Pillars

- In what ways could living by these Pillars improve our connection?
- Are aspects of the Pillars challenging or unclear?
- How can we help each other uphold these principles consistently?
- Are you ready to commit to living by these Pillars?

RESET:
Your emotional safe word

Moments when one of you strays from the Instructions or Pillars, consciously or not, are bound to happen. We're all works of art in progress. When it happens, think of 'Reset' as your emotional safe word—a simple, one-word signal that stops everything and shifts the focus to realignment in real-time.

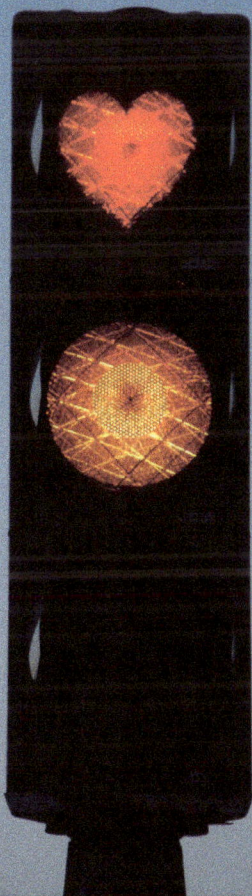

Reset

When you notice a deviation from the Instructions or Pillars, gently say "Reset." At that moment, you become Player 1.
Reset isn't an accusation—it's a shared cue to pause and recalibrate together.

Identify

Player 1 calmly states what prompted the Reset: "It seems like we moved away from [Instruction or Pillar]." The focus is on shared understanding, without assigning blame.

- **If Player 2 agrees**, they say, "I see why you felt that way. Here's why it happened, and what I'll do differently next time."
- **If Player 2 doesn't agree**, they respond, "I hear your perspective, but I see it differently. Here's what I was experiencing…" After that, if Player 1 still holds their point of view, Player 2 restates Player 1's point of view until they get a thumbs-up for understanding. Then switch roles: Player 1 restates Player 2's perspective until *they* get the thumbs-up.

Once both perspectives are understood, have a Truth Empowered Convo to explore how to navigate this kind of situation in the future.

Realign

When Identify is complete, both players repeat the Instruction or Pillar at the center of this Reset, like "Non-Meanness" or "Embrace the Power of Apology." (Player 2 goes first.)

Play

Just like resuming a movie after you've paused it, both players end the Reset process by simultaneously saying, "Play!" (And yes, the double meaning is intended.)

LEVEL

07

LET'S PLAY!

THE GAMES: PATHWAYS TO DEEPER CONNECTION

6 PAGES +
8 GAMES

What you will learn

You'll take your intimacy to the next level with these games, designed to spark interesting conversations, ignite vulnerability, and fine-tune emotional connection—all while having fun. Get ready for exciting challenges and surprising breakthroughs. Are you up for the challenge of going deeper? Let's play!

"NEVER UNDERESTIMATE THE *power* OF INTENTIONAL TIME WITH YOUR *partner.*"

—TERRY GASPARD

WHY PLAY
Games?

Sociologist Roger Caillois, in his book *Man, Play and Games,* said games serve no evolutionary purpose. Humans don't need games to survive. Yet games are a vital part of our social and spiritual development. Why?

Because they provide what life often doesn't: the security of rules, the thrill of winning, and the gift of fun. Playing games help societies hone social skills, experiment with roles, and explore relationships—all in a fun, low-stakes environment. Games also make us challenge ourselves to 'level up.'

The games here help you level up at conscious conversations. You've likely seen that learning this new language can feel forced, and diving into deeper emotional waters can feel tense. Games can put smiles on your faces while you grow. Why not *enjoy* learning to love yourselves and each other more deeply?

WHEN IT'S STRUCTURED AS A GAME, INTIMACY ISN'T WORK. IT'S PLAY.

The games of Truth Empowered Relationships ask you to invite extreme emotions, follow your curiosity, and practice radical honesty. They encourage you to lean into this new shared language, creating new patterns for trust and intimacy. They'll help you integrate Truth Empowered Convos into your everyday lives. And they can turn date nights into adventurous deep dives into each other's hearts.

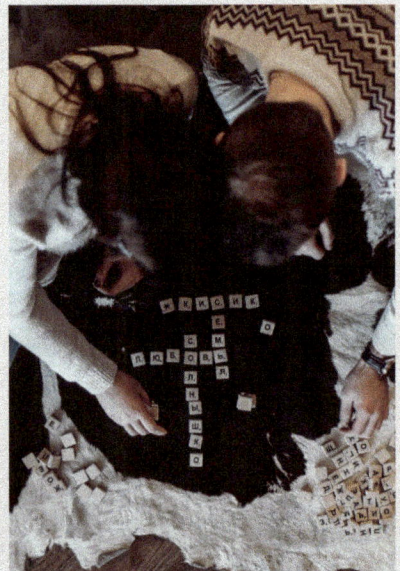

Who says intimacy can't be fun?

I used to be ultra-competitive when I played board games. Every particle of my being was focused on winning, looking for every angle, any advantage. Backgammon, *Monopoly, Clue*—I was unbeatable. What I didn't realize was, I was also insufferable.

Most people play games to relax. I played to cope with a lifetime of unresolved trauma. Coming out on top was life or death for me—and that's not a playful energy.

One night at my friend Rick's house, I put a *Trivial Pursuit* beatdown on a group of our friends. Victory was mine—but as the conversation carried on, I noticed everyone was turned away from me, talking to each other. No one wanted to engage with me.

Shocked, I wandered into the kitchen, found a piece of paper, and wrote this down:

IN THE JOY OF WINNING, I AM ALONE

On the concept of
WINNING
(FOR YOU COMPETITORS)

Winning puts you above all the rest—it sets you apart. But that also means **it separates you.** Look at it this way: has winning an argument with your partner ever brought you closer together?

I'm not the only ultra-competitive person out there. If you also play games to win, here's how to channel that drive into winning strategies for intimacy:

• *Who can drop the waterline lower?*
You'll be a generator of depth in convos.

• *What questions create the most depth?*
Your partner will open up in new ways.

• *Who will practice this shared language even when they don't feel like it?*
That athlete's will to *prepare* to win applies to mastering intimate convos.

Lastly: a good competitor knows the object of a game. Truth Empowered Relationships has at least three of them. Choose whichever one resonates the most, lights you up the most, speaks most to the competitor in you.

OBJECT OF THE GAME:
to not control your experience

OBJECT OF THE GAME:
to have fun as you grow as a human being and heal your relationship

OBJECT OF THE GAME:
to enjoy being in love

The best part? No matter which object you choose, you can't lose, because winning these games won't set you apart —it'll bring you closer.

INTERMEDIATE

CLOSENESS COUNTER

FOR TWO PLAYERS

SUGGESTED LENGTH
30-60 MINUTES

OBJECT OF THE GAME

Gauge the emotional closeness between you and your partner, while discovering how your words and nonverbal cues shape each other's experience of closeness.

HOW TO PLAY

Share: Player 1 sets a timer for two minutes and shares their stream authentically.

Move: During or after Player 1 shares, Player 2 moves closer or further away, based on how the share affects their sense of connection. Player 2 can move multiple times while they listen.

Explain: When Player 1's done, Player 2 shares why they moved.
- Example: "I moved closer because you were vulnerable" or "I moved back because I felt judged."

Clarify and Adjust: Player 1 may ask CQs about Player 2's move. Based on Player 2's answers, Player 1 may choose to move closer or further to reflect their state of connectedness.

Switch Roles: Player 2 shares for two minutes while Player 1 listens, moves, and explains their move.

Continue Alternating: Repeat until both players feel the conversation is complete. Max closeness is embracing at the center of the room or meeting in the middle of the game board. Max distance is one or both partners at the edge of the space.

Tips:
- If your partner reaches max distance, ask: "Is there something specific you're hoping to hear from me?" As your next convo, share your reactions to their answer.
- You may feel called to move based not just on your reactions to your partner's *words*, but also to their *moves*. Follow your instincts, and explain them when it's your turn.

INTERMEDIATE

SWITCH

FOR TWO PLAYERS

SUGGESTED LENGTH 10-15 MINUTES

OBJECT OF THE GAME

Sharpen your ability to truly understand someone else's perspective. This game turns misunderstandings into opportunities for connection, and shows how differences of opinion don't have to lead to conflict.

HOW TO PLAY

Pick a Topic: Choose a topic or situation where you might have differing views or emotions. It could be something small, like where to go for dinner, or something deeper, like how you each define success.

Player 1 Shares: Player 1 shares their perspective. Player 2's role is only to listen and ask clarifying questions (CQs), if any.

Player 2 Adopts the Viewpoint: Once Player 1 finishes, Player 2 'steps into their shoes' and expresses Player 1's perspective as if it were their own, trying to convey Player 1's point of view as accurately as possible.

Refine Understanding: If Player 1 didn't feel their perspective was fully captured, they reframe their thoughts in new words. Player 2 tries again until Player 1 gives a thumbs-up.

Change Roles: Change roles and repeat—Player 2 now shares their perspective, and Player 1 takes on the challenge of embodying and articulating it until they get a thumbs-up.

Celebrate Your Connection: Congratulations! Understanding another person's perspective, even temporarily, takes courage and empathy. By doing it, you've strengthened your emotional intelligence (EQ)—and your bond.

PAUSE

OBJECT OF THE GAME

Stop conversations from spiraling out of control. The aim is to catch missteps early, reflect on what caused them, and reset the dialogue with more clarity and without harming connection.

HOW TO PLAY

Call a Pause: When a conversation starts feeling heated, elevated, confusing, or unproductive, either partner can say "Pause." This immediately stops the conversation, and the person who called it becomes Player 1.

Player 1 Reflects: Player 1 has 15 seconds to begin reflecting on where they believe the conversation began to derail and why, looking for *their* responsibility in the derailment, like:
- "I think things went sideways when I brought up work. It might've sounded like I was criticizing you."
- "When I asked that question, I assumed from your tone that you were angry, and I got defensive."

If Player 1 doesn't begin voicing their stream within 15 seconds, the convo resumes where it left off.

Player 2 Reflects: If Player 2 doesn't agree that the convo was derailing, proceed to the next step. If they do agree, Player 2 then looks for and voices *their* responsibility.

Rewind and Reset: Player 1 says "Rewind," signaling a restart from just before the identified misstep. Both players can now choose a different way to express themselves.

Press 'Play:' With the air cleared and new awareness in place, both players say 'Play!' and the conversation picks back up where it left off.

WHY THIS WORKS: Pausing interrupts reactive patterns and brings mindfulness into the conversation. By reflecting and reframing, you reduce emotional escalation and build trust.

AND WHAT ELSE?

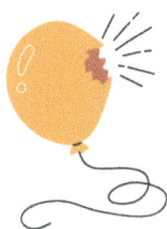

OBJECT OF THE GAME

To uncover and release layers of unspoken resentments in a safe, neutral space. Resentments are the single most powerful block to intimacy; releasing them can lead to renewed closeness and openness.

HOW TO PLAY

Set a Timer: Set a timer for 10 minutes. Player 1 shares their resentments, starting each sentence with, "I resent you for..." Examples:
- "I resent you for not listening to me last night."
- "I resent you for making vacation plans without talking to me first."

Respond with Neutrality: After each resentment, Player 2 simply responds, "And what else?" This encourages Player 1 to uncover deeper layers of unspoken feelings—including resentments they didn't even realize were there.

Switch Roles: After Player 1 has finished, switch roles. Player 2 now becomes the one to share their resentments, while Player 1 responds with "And what else?"

If There's Nothing Else: The game ends when the time's up, or Player 1's expressed everything they needed to say.

Tips for Success:
- *Neutrality Matters: Player 2 stays neutral while listening, no matter how challenging it feels. When roles switch, Player 1 practices the same nonjudgmental listening.*
- *Allow Natural Transformation: As resentments are released, they may evolve into appreciations. If this happens, include them—like "I appreciate you for being patient with me." The listener still responds with "And what else?" to maintain the flow.*

BOMB SQUAD

FOR TWO PLAYERS

**SUGGESTED LENGTH
45 MINUTES**

OBJECT OF THE GAME

Work together to tackle charged or unresolved issues within a set time frame, all while staying true to the Instructions and Pillars. Facing stressors consciously as a couple builds resilience and promotes quicker, healthier conflict resolution.

HOW TO PLAY

Identify the Bomb: Agree on a sensitive topic—one you've been avoiding, a recurring argument, or an unresolved issue. Set a timer for 45 minutes.

Defuse Mode: Have a Truth Empowered Convo with the goal of lowering the emotional charge. Take turns expressing your perspectives, listening deeply, asking thoughtful questions, and responding with intention.

- Keep the conversation concise: focus on 'protein words' (essential and meaningful) and cut out the 'empty carbs' (unnecessary filler).
- If things get elevated, use the Reset process before continuing.

If You Defused the Bomb: If you find mutual harmony, celebrate your teamwork! Reflect on what worked, share insights, and solidify any agreements you've made.

If the Bomb 'Went Off:' If the timer goes off before you reach harmony, don't worry—bomb squads wear protective gear for moments like this. Here's yours:

- Celebrate the Effort: Facing an explosive topic consciously for 45 minutes is an achievement in itself.
- Reflect Together: Discuss what got elevated, where progress was made (even small wins), and what you respected about your partner's effort in the conversation.
- Plan for Next Time: Commit to trying again with fresh insights. Every bomb can be defused with patience, respect, and mutual effort—it just might take a few tries.

NAKED NARRATIVES

**SUGGESTED LENGTH
2-3 HOURS**

OBJECT OF THE GAME

Practice neutrality while you explore each other's sexual histories. This game creates a safe space for openness, honesty and deep connection around a subject that's often kept hidden.

HOW TO PLAY

Get Comfy: Agree on a space. Have a notebook or device handy for taking notes. Set an intention for openness, curiosity, and non-judgment. Rock Paper Scissors: winner is Player 1.

Player 1, share your complete sexual history, including:
- Enjoyable and unenjoyable experiences
- Desires and fantasies
- Self-pleasure history
- Unwanted or traumatic experiences

Be as open as you feel safe being. Clothing is optional: if you're comfortable, sharing unclothed can heighten intimacy.

Player 2, listen neutrally: Notice any jealousy, discomfort, or insecurity, but focus on listening with curiosity. Remind yourself that your partner's history is part of their timeline, and doesn't define or diminish your relationship. Take notes if needed, and say "pause" if a moment feels overwhelming.

Ask and Reflect:

After Player 1 finishes, Player 2 asks CQs: "What was that like for you?" and "How has that affected intimacy for you?" Then, for up to 3 minutes, Player 2 shares their inner stream about what they heard, including personal insights and feelings. **Jealousy is normal**, but beneath it often lies **insecurity**. Leaning into both with awareness can help neutralize their power.

Switch Roles: Player 2 now shares; Player 1 listens and reflects.

Have a Truth Empowered Convo: Discuss what you learned, how it affects your connection, and what it reveals about your boundaries, desires, and future intimacy.

ADVANCED

RECORD-A-FIGHT

FOR TWO PLAYERS

SUGGESTED LENGTH 2-3 HOURS

OBJECT OF THE GAME

Turn heated arguments into opportunities for deeper understanding and emotional healing. Learn to spot your communication patterns and emotional triggers, and to uncover the misunderstandings that fuel conflict.

HOW TO PLAY

Agree to Disagree—on Record: Before tensions rise, make a pact: the next time a conversation starts to escalate, let it play out naturally—but with one rule: **record it**. Think of it as a chance to catch your unfiltered communication in action.

Press 'Record:' When emotions begin to climb, one partner hits record. Let the argument unfold as it normally would—no censoring, even if it's messy and raw and 'unconscious.'

Schedule Playback: Once the storm settles, agree on a time to listen to the recording together. As you replay the conversation, either of you can hit the 'pause' button to:
- **Re-say**: If what you said didn't align with the Instructions or Pillars, restate it so it does. For instance, shift blame-filled statements into ownership of your emotions.
- **Uncover the Roots**: Pinpoint where things went off track. Look for misunderstandings, assumptions, or triggers.

Spot Patterns and Triggers: While you listen, look for recurring communication habits, emotional cues, or assumptions. Recognizing these can help you sidestep future conflicts.

Share Insights: Once you've gone through the recording, each partner shares what they've learned—about themselves, their triggers, and their dynamic as a couple.

TIP:
Use the recording as a tool for growth, not to find out who was 'right' or to 'win' the argument.

THE END

FOR TWO PLAYERS

**SUGGESTED LENGTH
2 HOURS**

OBJECT OF THE GAME

To understand your and your partner's emotions surrounding the end of life in human form. You'll get to express, with openness and love, what might otherwise go unsaid when the end's actually near, bringing clarity, peace, and a sense of togetherness to one of life's most profound experiences.

HOW TO PLAY

Find the Right Space: Choose a setting where you feel safe and uninterrupted. Before you begin, ground yourselves in why you're doing this: to face life's final chapter with honesty, courage, and connection.

Start with Your Internal Weather Report: Rock Paper Scissors; winner goes first. Each of you first shares what it feels like to have this conversation. Express any nerves, hopes, or intentions, and set a tone of empathy and authenticity.

Pick a Prompt: Take turns exploring these prompts—or create your own as the conversation flows:
- "What would you choose as your last meal?"
- "Which memories would you want to relive or share?"
- "If you had one final message to me, what would it be?"
- "What would you want my last words to you to be?"

Embrace Emotions: Tears, laughter, or silence—whatever emotions or reactions come up, let them all exist. Simply be present with each other.

Reflect Together: Close by discussing what this experience revealed. Share any feelings, insights, or words of love and gratitude. Let this be a moment of mutual appreciation for the time you share now—and always.

Imagine standing in a hall of mirrors. Each reflection warps reality, distorting what you know to be true. That's what being lied to over and over does—it distorts your world, undermines your instincts, and fractures your sense of what's real. Lies don't just deceive; they disorient. They create a fog in their wake, leaving you adrift from your own inner stream.

Truth cuts through the fog, and realigns us with what's real. Truth soothes our nervous system and boosts our self-confidence, because it validates our intuition. Truthful connections can withstand conflict, because they're built on respect, not shifting sand. Truth is the antidote to the doubt and self-betrayal our psyches form when we're repeatedly lied to.

Remember the story of the emperor's new clothes? It took the honesty of a child to reconnect people with their own senses, so they could see the truth right in front of them. Truth reconnects people to themselves. Societies rooted in truth have the strength to confront injustices and correct imbalances. Truth can transform even the most fractured spaces into places of healing and hope.

But **truth requires bravery.**

So let us be brave. Let truth be our medicine—in our partnerships, our families, and our communities. Let us make truth our guiding principle. Without it, we're stumbling along in darkness, vulnerable to manipulation and mistreatment. With it, we see our world clearly, act boldly, and create enduring and fulfilling bonds.

Let truth light our path forward.

a final word on truth.

MAY THE *Truth* SET YOU FREE

You've become fluent in the language of you. Stay with it, even when it's tough. The real love you get in a Truth Empowered Relationship is worth the effort.

By choosing a Truth Empowered Relationship, you're not just transforming your own love story—you're contributing to the evolution of authentic love on this planet. Each step you take toward deeper connection through conscious communication ripples outward, inspiring others to love with honesty and courage.

Remember: the path to real, meaningful love isn't always smooth. When challenges arise, revisit the Instructions and the Pillars. Let them guide you back to the core of your relationship. And if you ever feel stuck or unsure, you're not alone; Heather and I are ready to be your neutral, nonjudgemental 'referees' whenever you need us.

We're rooting for you both.

Marshall and Heather

The object of
Truth Empowered
Relationships
is to *enjoy*
being in love.

Acknowledgements

To Rick, for your personal growth companionship, for your friendship, for your aid, and for gifting me with so much life-changing transformational education.

To David, for being my friend before and after I stood for the truth, and for being perhaps the most supportive human I've ever known.

To Clay, for always being willing to go there with me. Your authenticity and commitment to respectfulness are consistent, unshakable and inspiring.

To Barbara, for your willingness to have the Truth Empowered Convos that transformed our relationship; for your non-judgmental listening when I needed it; and for your constant generosity that's given my family the chance to rewrite our story.

To Westley: your trust empowered me; your friendship has lit up my life. Every day, I learn from you and laugh with you. I'm so lucky to be able to call you son.

M.

thank you

GLOSSARY

The following pages are an overview of the neuroscientific and psychological terms mentioned in this book—as well as several terms unique to Truth Empowered Relationships.

When we're in love, the neural machinery that critically assesses others—including our partners—can shut down. So love really can be blind. But understanding the neuroscience behind it can help you 'see' again.

Acute stress response

Our brain's survival toolkit offers us five options: **fight** (actively confront the threat), **flight** (escape the danger), **freeze** (momentary paralysis or indecision), **fawn** (people-please to avoid harm), and **flop** (give up completely).

Amygdala

This almond-shaped brain structure is your emotional radar: it alerts you and activates you in the face of danger —real or perceived. It's key to understanding triggers and cultivating emotional safety in relationships.

Anger spectrum

Like a rainbow, anger spans from mild annoyance to full-blown rage. Along the way are shades of the anger spectrum: frustration, irritation, resentment, indignation —even fury. Understanding these can help diffuse conflict before it escalates.

Anterior Cingulate Cortex (ACC)

This part of your brain is like air traffic control for emotions and decisions. It helps you juggle empathy, focus and self-control, to make sure your feelings and actions 'play nice together.'

GLOSSARY

Autonomic nervous system

Your body's behind-the-scenes operator, managing automatic functions like breathing and heart rate. It has two modes: **sympathetic** (fight-or-flight, energizing you in times of stress) and **parasympathetic** (rest-and-digest, calming you back down).

Basal ganglia

Your brain's habit hub, it stores routines you've practiced over and over, like riding a bike, brushing your teeth—or reacting habitually in conversations. It's your internal 'muscle memory' manager, shaping your daily patterns and reactions.

CQs

Clarifying Questions (when you're unsure about something) and Curious Questions (when you're genuinely curious). CQs can clear up confusion and spark deeper understanding—and they show you're truly listening.

Cognitive bias

Your brain loves shortcuts, but sometimes those shortcuts can lead you astray. Cognitive bias is your mind tricking you into seeing the world in a way that confirms what you already believe—whether it's true or not.

Cognitive dissonance

That uncomfortable feeling when your actions or beliefs clash, like an honest person telling a little white lie. It's your brain's nudge to sort out the disconnect and realign with your values.

GLOSSARY

Cognitive distancing

Stepping back from your inner world to see it more clearly—without getting swept up in it. This deliberate separation helps you respond thoughtfully instead of reacting impulsively, so convos stay calm and intentional.

Cognitive flexibility

Your brain's version of adaptability, this means you're able to shift your thinking when faced with new ideas or challenges. It's a relationship superpower for navigating change and staying open to possibilities.

Codependency

When you care so much about someone else's feelings that you forget about your own. It's like losing yourself in their story. Healthy relationships happen when you learn to show up for both them *and* yourself.

Come-froms

The "why" behind someone's words or actions—the thoughts, feelings or experiences that shape where they're coming from. When you understand someone's come-from, it's easier to really connect.

Confirmation bias

Your brain playing favorites with information: it only notices what proves you right—and ignores what doesn't. It's sneaky, but catching it helps you stay open-minded and have fairer conversations.

GLOSSARY

Cortisol

Known as the stress hormone, cortisol kicks in when you're feeling overwhelmed or under pressure. It's useful in small doses, but in relationships, too much cortisol can make it hard to think clearly or respond calmly. Managing it helps you stay present and connected.

Default Mode Network (DMN)

The brain's "idle mode" kicks in when you're daydreaming or reflecting. It's where self-awareness and big-picture thinking happen. Tuning into your DMN helps you process emotions and gain insights that can deepen relationships.

Dopamine

The brain's reward chemical, dopamine gives you a little buzz when something feels good, like solving a problem—or connecting with someone you care about. It's the spark that keeps motivation and relationships thriving.

Earned secure attachment

It's learning to feel safe and steady in relationships, even if you didn't start out that way. By working through past hurts and building trust with others, you create the kind of connection where you can truly relax and be yourself.

Emotional attunement

The art of deeply sensing and responding to another's emotions. When you're emotionally attuned, you can sense what someone's going through, and respond in a way that shows you really get them.

GLOSSARY

Emotional Intelligence (EQ)

Being skilled with feelings: knowing what's going on inside you and picking up on what others are feeling too. EQ helps you handle emotions like a pro and connect with people in a real, meaningful way.

Insula

Your brain's feelings translator. It links your emotions to physical sensations, like that gut twist when you're nervous. Tuning into your insula can help you understand yourself and others on a deeper level.

Interbrain synchrony

When you truly connect with someone, your brains sync up—like two musicians improving perfectly without sheet music. The flow of understanding feels almost instinctive.

Limbic system

Your brain's emotional HQ, it handles things like fear, joy, memory—and survival. It's the part of you that feels before you think: your raw emotions before logic kicks in.

Metacognition

It's thinking about how you think—like having a conversation with your own brain. This superpower helps you catch unhelpful patterns and grow in relationships.

Mirror neurons

Like emotional mirrors, mirror neurons light up when you see someone laugh, cry, or yawn, helping you feel what they're feeling. They're the secret behind empathy.

●●●

GLOSSARY

Neuroplasticity

Your brain's ability to rewire itself—it's like upgrading your mental software. With effort and practice, you can change old habits, heal emotional patterns, and build healthier ways of thinking and relating.

Neuronal pathways

The brain's highways of habit and thought. Strengthening positive pathways and weakening negative ones transforms how you relate to yourself and others.

Oxytocin

The bonding hormone. It's released through touch, affection and trust, making relationships feel warm and safe. Oxytocin is nature's intimacy glue.

Parasympathetic nervous system

Your body's 'chill mode,' this system helps you relax, digest, and recover. It's like pressing the reset button, so you can feel calm and balanced again.

Pattern recognition

Your brain's knack for spotting connections and recurring themes, like noticing the same argument keeps happening. Recognizing patterns helps you break unhelpful cycles and make more thoughtful choices in relationships.

Prefrontal cortex

Your brain's CEO, the prefrontal cortex is like your inner coach, helping you plan, focus, manage impulses—and respond thoughtfully instead of reacting in tough convos.

● ● ●

GLOSSARY

Reticular Activating System (RAS)

Your brain's focus filter, decides what gets your attention —like spotting every blue car after you buy one. Training your RAS helps you look for opportunities and solutions.

Speaking to your resistance

Giving voice to the fears, doubts, or hesitations that hold you back. By sharing The Under, you bring hidden struggles into the open, making it easier to move forward.

Stream

The unfiltered flow of your inner narrative. Paying attention to your stream can uncover insights that help you understand what's really driving your reactions.

Theory of mind

The idea that others have their own thoughts, feelings, and perspectives. Like stepping into someone else's shoes, theory of mind helps avoid misunderstandings.

Triggers

Emotional landmines tied to unresolved past experiences. When something triggers you, it's a chance to uncover old wounds and grow,

Unwinding

Giving yourself—or someone else—the freedom to simply express your or their inner world without structure. No fixing, no advice, just a quiet space for untangling thoughts and letting answers naturally surface.

www.ingramcontent.com/pod-product-compliance
Lightning Source LLC
Chambersburg PA
CBHW041828280326
41926CB00105B/4687